DATE DUE

ACTON, GLADSTONE AND OTHERS

ACTON, GLADSTONE AND OTHERS

BY

MARY DREW (Gladstone)

Essay Index Reprint Series

BOOKS FOR LIBRARIES PRESS, INC.
FREEPORT, NEW YORK

First published 1924
Reprinted 1968

LIBRARY OF CONGRESS CATALOG CARD NUMBER:

68-20294

CONTENTS

CONTENTS

My thanks are due to the Editors of the *Fortnightly Review* and the *Nineteenth Century*, who have allowed me to reproduce some of the material on which this book is based. Also to Messrs. Macmillan for giving me permission to quote from Lord Morley's "Recollections," and to the Executors of Sir E. Cook for letting me quote some passages from "The Life of John Ruskin." And to Mr. Walter de la Mare for giving me the use of Dr. Holland's poem "Lyrical Rhapsody."

ACTON, GLADSTONE AND OTHERS

CHAPTER I

ACTON AND GLADSTONE[1]

"ALL I write, and all I think, and all I hope, is based on the Divinity of Our Lord—the one central hope of our poor wayward race."

This was the impregnable rock upon which Mr. Gladstone's life was founded, and if we look through the letters and writings of Lord Acton we shall find the same note sounded throughout. It was of little moment to which branch of the Holy Catholic Church—the Anglo-Catholic or the Roman Catholic —the two men belonged. That which divided them was small indeed compared with that which united them. Both were Catholic in the deepest and widest sense of the term, both were conscious and proud of their membership in the Apostolic and Universal Church, " patriot citizens of the Kingdom of God " —their zeal for the Church transcended patriotism— it is seen throughout their lives and deeds. Both were staunch believers in religious liberty, and both were

[1] I am greatly indebted to those who have studied the life of Lord Acton—Mr. J. Neville Figgis, Mr. Herbert Paul, Mr. G. P. Gooch, Lady Blennerhassett, Mr. L. March Phillipps, and to Lord Morley.

possessed of a deep longing for the reunion of Christendom. In all the essentials of our faith they were in sympathy ; in fundamentals they were identical. Both were profound believers in the truth of Christianity ; both drew their inspiration from the same deep source. No men of their day were more learned in all that touched their faith ; few could have approached their mental and moral stature. No men more earnestly and ardently practised the truth by which they lived ; they bore witness by their unostentatious, consistent lives to the faith that was within them.

Their relations strengthened with time and intercourse. It was Matthew Arnold who said " Gladstone influences all around him but Acton. It is Acton who influences Gladstone." In truth, they acted and reacted on one another. Both were ever conscious of those things of the Spirit which at once purify and ennoble human nature. In Mr. Gladstone Lord Acton saw fulfilled the idea that politics is an affair of morality, that it touches eternal interests and eternal standards as much as vices and virtues in private life.

Politics to Lord Acton were nearer religion, party was more like a Church, error more like heresy, prejudice like sin, than is to be found with most politicians. To a friend he once described Mr. Gladstone as one who treated politics on the largest scale as the art of doing what is right. In 1881 Lord Acton spoke of the peace with the Boers as the noblest work of the Ministry. He rejoiced over this " victory with heartier joy and a purer pride than I have been able to feel at any public event since I broke my heart over the surrender of Lee."

What gave the act, in his eyes, its moral significance was the courage which inspired the British Government to complete the negotiations—started before the Majuba disaster—in the teeth of that defeat. It is easy enough to be magnanimous to a fallen foe, but to be magnanimous at the moment of victory is as rare among nations as among individuals ; it is a degree of morality so lofty as seldom to be attained in the one as in the other. In truth, in some cases, defeat is a greater triumph than victory.

Possibly, the most notable occasions on which Mr. Gladstone stood in the House of Commons pouring out the passion of his soul on behalf of liberty—to be defeated at the moment, to triumph in the end—would be his speech on the Franchise in April, 1866, his speech on the Eastern Question, May, 1877, and his speech on Home Rule for Ireland in April, 1886.

Mr. Gladstone and Lord Acton each had qualities of character and intellect which specially appealed to the other, both gathered vast knowledge from their studies, Lord Acton especially, of all people alive or dead who really count in this world. Both were born students, learners to the end of their lives. In the last conversation with his son, Lord Acton solemnly adjured him not to judge so severely as he himself had judged, but " to make allowance for human weakness." By this last admission he showed that he, who dedicated his life to the pursuit of truth, was learning to the very end. In three things they believed with all their strength : liberty, truth and the moral law. Lord Acton would not allow the least qualification in the supremacy of any one of them. He was unflinching in his condemnation of anything that infringed on the truth—he staked his all on the whole, undiluted and absolute truth. To him and Mr. Gladstone religion was the most supreme of interests. It was the habit of their minds. It was the guiding star of their lives.

Attraction to each other must have been enhanced by contrast in life occupations. The effect of intercourse, as might be expected—the one mainly a man of action, the other mainly a man of ideas—must have been calming to the one and stimulating to the other. To both men the past was a thing of profound significance, for they had an abiding reverence for all that was ancient and ordered, though no men could have listened more carefully to the Spirit of the Age. They united a profound reverence for the past with an intense faith in the future.

They believed in evolution and progress. " We have no thread through the enormous intricacy of politics, except the idea of progress towards more perfect freedom and the divine right of free men." " Liberty is the sign and the motive and the prize in the upward and onward advance of the race."

They both nourished a deep affection and admiration for Dr. Döllinger, that " glory of Catholic learning," as he has been called. Acton was but a boy of eleven when Mr. Gladstone, at the age of thirty-five, paid his first visit to the great master. During the two or three days he was at Munich their intercourse must have lasted many hours. I understand it was on this occasion that, after supper, they sat talking far into the night. So engrossed were they with the enthralling nature of their conversation, that the small hours of the morning passed unheeded, and it was not until the servant entered the room to let in the new day that the two men separated.

Acton lived with Dr. Döllinger from 1849 to 1855, the laws of the English universities being then too narrow to admit of any other than Church of England undergraduates. His descent, on the one side, from the Acton who was Prime Minister in the Kingdom of Naples, during the Napoleonic era, and from the great house of Dalberg on the other, brought him into a wide and cultivated circle, and this was enhanced by his mother's marriage with Lord Gran-

ville. The best, not only of British, but of European
society and learning was at his command.

The first letter he received from Mr. Gladstone
was written in 1859. Mr. Gladstone had read the
Acton article, written at the age of twenty-five, on
John Stuart Mill. " I have read your remarkable
and valuable paper," he wrote. " Its principles and
politics I embrace ; its research and wealth of knowledge I admire ; and its whole atmosphere is that
which I desire to breathe." A moving declaration
from a statesman of fifty to a student of twenty-
five.

In reading, Lord Acton was a gourmet, Mr. Gladstone a gourmand : the younger man often deplored
the lack of selection in Mr. Gladstone's reading and
the catholicity of his tastes. It would not be true
to say that Lord Acton, like many others, was not
sometimes perplexed by certain aspects of Mr.
Gladstone's mind.

In more than one of the later phases of his life [he wrote
in a letter I received from him in 1881] I fancy you hardly
recognised the secret laws of the growth of his mind, and
join him, sometimes by an effort, over a gap—anybody can
be on his side who waits to be under the thrall of his speech.
The difficulty is to hear the grass growing, to know the road
by which he travels, the description of engine, the quality of
the stuff he treats with, the stars he steers by.[1]

---

[1] " Letters to Mary Gladstone."

Both had a rare sense of fitness, of proportion, of harmony, which kept them from wasting time and trouble on the things that do not matter. With Lord Action what to refuse or neglect became a fine art. He studied facts, not so much as facts, as in their relation to principles ; the thoughts and ideas of men were to him often more important than their deeds ; the range and exactness of his knowledge was as varied as it was profound. To him history and philosophy were one. Though his knowledge of history penetrated far back into the past, he also mastered the whole field of history of recent times, specially in the Reformation and Renaissance periods, including older theology and modern Biblical criticism and research. To a boundless knowledge of books Lord Acton added an un-rivalled knowledge of men. His passion for know-ledge, no doubt, checked his powers of production. His " History of Liberty," it has been aptly said, " is the greatest book that never was written." [1]

In 1880 the present writer ventured to call Lord Acton's attention to " The Madonna of the Future," a story recently written by Henry James—a story in which the artist dreamed, throughout his life, of the wonderful picture he was going to paint. After his death, when his studio is entered, a blank canvas is discovered upon the easel. From this time

[1] " Europe Unbound."   L. March Phillipps.

Lord Acton used this title in his letters to me referring to his own work. Both Newman and Döllinger had prophesied that if he wrote no great book
before he was forty his vast erudition would paralyse
his powers of expression. Not one page of the actual
" History of Liberty " was ever written. But in his
lectures, reviews, and letters, texts are to be found
upon which whole treatises or books might be written
on this greatest of subjects. At Bridgnorth, in 1877,
he gave the main ideas of his projected work in two
remarkable lectures on Freedom.[1]

The words Lord Acton wrote about Burke may
well be applied to himself :—

Systems of scientific thought have been built up by famous
scholars on fragments that fell from his table. Great literary
fortunes have been made by men who traded on the hun-
dredth part of him. Brougham and Lowe lived by the
vitality of his ideas. Mackintosh and Macaulay are only
Burke trimmed and stripped of all that touched the skies.[2]

No man can ever measure the effect of Acton's
life. That which he gave to the world in his character,
his thoughts and his example is greater than any
written book. The life he lived was the book he
wrote.

That low man seeks a little thing to do,
    Sees it and does it.
This high man with a great thing to pursue
    Dies ere he knows it.

[1] Lectures on " Freedom," etc.
[2] " Letters to Mary Gladstone."

That low man goes on adding one to one,
  His hundred's soon hit.
This high man, aiming at a million,
  Misses an unit.[1]

He " hitched his wagon to the stars."

One bit of personal experience may perhaps be
related here. From Tegernsee, where we stayed in
1879, we went on to Venice. Here I had the in-
estimable privilege and delight of seeing (for the first
time) Venice and its priceless treasures under Lord
Acton's supreme guidance. I can never forget the
intoxication of the first night in the Piazza of St.
Mark's, the music, the moonlight, the stir of the
crowd, the unparalleled beauty of the buildings.
But it is another evening that stands out chiefly in
my memory, an evening spent with Lord Acton on
the Piazzetta. It was a setting of unearthly beauty,
the silver rays of the moon shining upon the water,
and illuminating the classic lines of palaces and
churches.

The conversation turned on liberty, and the flood-
gates were unloosed :

With a passion and enthusiasm I have never heard
equalled, Lord Acton poured forth for us his own " History
of Liberty "—he let loose the long pent-up treasures of his
inmost soul. He spoke like a man inspired, as if, from

---

[1] " A Grammarian's Funeral."

some mountain summit high in air he saw beneath him the far-winding path of human progress from dim Cimmerian shores of prehistoric shadow, into the fuller yet broken and fitful light of the modern time. The eloquence was splendid ; yet greater than the eloquence was the penetrating vision which discerned through all events, and in all ages, the play of those moral forces, now creating, now destroying, always transmuting, which had moulded and remoulded human institutions and had given to the human spirit its ceaselessly changing forms of energy. It was as if the whole landscape of history had been suddenly lit up by a burst of sunlight.

I cannot do better than quote these memorable words used by Lord Bryce, for the words spoken to us seem to have been almost identically the same as those spoken to him ; but with Lord Bryce it was for six or seven minutes only, with us (my brother Herbert and me) it must have been a whole hour or more.

All through that memorable evening two figures tramped up and down the Piazzetta in front of us— the Crown Princess, afterwards Empress of Germany, and M. Renan. Often I have wondered whether, had they known what was taking place, they would not have given the world to share in our thrilling experience.

Mr. Gladstone was once heard to remark that if all the wits of man were to be united in one brain, that man would be unable to appraise with perfect justice any single moral action :

The shades of the rainbow [he wrote] are not so nice, the sands of the seashore are not such a multitude, as are the subtle, shifting, blending forms of thought and of circumstances that go to determine the character of one act. But there is One that seeth plainly and judgeth righteously.

And Lord Acton was the same in recognising the perplexity and complexity of moral problems :

So complex are they that almost every act can be honestly seen in different lights, and I can imagine so strong a case against our policy in Africa as to drive from his moorings any man not anchored in justice.

Both these men, while uncompromising in their condemnation of any offence against the moral law, would make every allowance for the offender. " Be true to your own beliefs and gracious towards those that dispute them."

With all the splendour of his gifts Mr. Gladstone was possessed by an overmastering love of goodness. The conclusions summed up by Lord Morley in the chapter called " Characteristics " [1]—possibly the masterpiece of his great Biography—must rest on the bedrock of the Diaries kept by Mr. Gladstone. These Diaries, forty small volumes of compressed handwriting, are concentrated evidence of his belief, habit, purpose, practice and performance—a stern,

[1] Morley's " Life of Gladstone," Vol. I., p. 218.

uncompromising record of daily work, done or not done—an unsparing introspective analysis of motive and conduct. His thoughts, his time, his deeds, his soul, were possessed by the inviolable obligation of moral duty. Scrupulously kept throughout his life, these Diaries record an abiding conviction of Divine guidance. He must often have been the despair of his colleagues in a Cabinet Council, for he brought every question, every problem, to the touchstone of conscience. He strove to apply the noble moralities of his creed to the affairs of his own nation, and, further, of the Commonwealth of Nations. Yet, in watching and guiding public opinion, as Lord Morley has observed, in feeling the pulse of the Cabinet or the House of Commons or the public, in appealing to the heart or soothing the mind of a colleague, he always kept before him the conviction that in political life you must be prepared to *do what you can, not what you want*, to act when you can, not when you would, and that as much wisdom is required in the choice of time and occasion as in the choice of policy. He fulfilled, to the best of his ability, the counsel of Marcus Aurelius, " Be content with ever so small an advance, and look even on that as a gain worth having."

It was " in the great and sinful streets of Naples as he passed," in the year 1832, at the age of twenty-two, that Mr. Gladstone underwent an experience, almost a revelation, which recalls the light given to St. Paul on the road to Damascus.

One Sunday, May 13th [he wrote in his Diary] something, I know not what, set me to examining the Occasional Offices of the Church in the Prayer Book. . . . I had previously taken a great deal of teaching direct from the Bible, but now the figure of the Church rose before me as a teacher, too, and I gradually found in how incomplete a manner I had drawn Divine truth from the sacred volume. . . . Such, for I believe I have given the fact as it occurred, in its silence and its solitude, was my first introduction to the august conception of the Church of Christ.

It presented to me Christianity under an aspect in which I had not yet known it : its ministry of simplicity, its channels of grace, its unending line of teachers, joining from the Head ; the sublime construction, based throughout upon historical fact, uplifting the idea of the community in which we live and of the access which it enjoys, through the new and living way, to the Presence of the Most High.

Up to that time Mr. Gladstone had been brought up in an exceedingly narrow creed ; it obliged him to believe that salvation depended absolutely on the literal acceptance of its tenets. " But long, long have I cast those weeds behind me," he wrote to Mr. Darbishire (December, 1862). His life had been fashioned on most austere lines, but from the moment of revelation recorded above, religion took on a very different meaning. He realised the neces-

sity of a system, a framework for anything that has
to endure. From this time he looked upon doctrine
or dogma as " the skeleton, the bones, that carried
the flesh, the blood, the life of the blessed thing we
call the Christian religion."

Lord Acton, in referring to his own Church,
wrote : " Our faith should stand, not on the virtues
of men, but on the surer ground of an institution and
a guidance that are divine." Though he belonged to
a Church, " whose communion to him was dearer
than life," he would frankly confess that there were
many acts as well as opinions, " not only sanctioned,
but enforced, by the authorities of the Church of
Rome, to which none could adhere without peril to
the soul."

An ardent Catholic, Lord Action was also an
ardent Liberal, who confessed to the necessity of
removing everything in Catholicism incompatible
with liberty, and everything in politics incompatible
with Catholicism. In Mr. Gladstone Lord Acton
discerned a knight-errant of freedom.[1] Having
known Mr. Gladstone from his youth upwards, and
from the inside, he realised the simplicity as well as
the greatness of his character ; he perceived that he
had no object except " to learn what was true, and to
do what was right." Lord Acton has been truly
called " the most hypercritical of men, the precise

---

[1] " Lord Acton's Correspondence."

opposite of a hero-worshipper, an iconoclast, if ever there was one, who yet regarded Mr. Gladstone as the first of English statesmen, *living or dead*." [1]

As has been said, Lord Acton recognised in his hero the union of principle and policy. He knew the three sources from which Mr. Gladstone's character drew its inspiration ; his three channels of grace—the Bible, the Church, and the conscience. To Bishop Creighton Lord Acton once wrote : " Remember that nearly all great men are bad men." Such was his conviction of the deteriorating effect of power. " Power is poison." [2] In Mr. Gladstone, notwithstanding the overmastering temptations of almost limitless power, he witnessed the steadfastness and serenity of his soul. The close relations between the two men did infinite honour to them both—the strength of their affection never blinded their eyes. Freedom and frankness, clear as crystal, reigned between them : Lord Acton never shrank from criticising Mr. Gladstone. Mr. Gladstone invited his criticism, and always welcomed even his condemnation, as a sincere proof of his friendship.

In the three great departments of human thought —theological, historical and philosophical—in the literature that set them forth, they were closely

[1] Herbert Paul's Introduction to Lord Acton's " Letters to Mary Gladstone."
[2] Fénelon.

allied ; their common interest in the great masters, Plato and Aristotle, Dante and Thomas Aquinas, Butler and Burke, drew them together. In the libraries they collected, in the spirit in which they selected them, there was a striking, a characteristic sympathy—St. Deiniol's Library at Hawarden and the Acton Library at Cambridge. The former consists of two large rooms, each with a gallery, one room for Divinity, the other for Humanity, presented to the students of Great Britain for the promotion of Divine Learning.

Divine learning [Mr. Gladstone wrote], in order to reach the highest efficacy, has been, and ought to be, associated with the various branches of human knowledge, especially with History and Philosophy. The great question of belief is, in the main, the first concern of the human race.

All understanding of history depends [wrote Lord Acton] on one's understanding the forces that make it, and religious forces are the most active and the most definite. To develop and perfect and arm conscience is the great achievement of history, the chief business of every life, and the first agent therein is religion.

Let us take a few nuggets from Lord Acton's and Mr. Gladstone's writings or speeches and one or two of their favourite texts.

The first lesson of history is that liberty depends on the division of power.

The danger is not that a particular class is unfit to govern— every class is unfit to govern.

True liberty depends on the multiplicity of checking forces.

Imagine a congress of celebrities, such as More, Bacon, Grotius, Pascal, Cromwell, Bossuet, Montesquieu, Jefferson, Napoleon, Pitt—the result would be an Encyclopædia of Error.

Liberty depends on the union of innumerable conditions which embrace the entire life of man.

Nations that are without the self-governing force of religion are unfit for freedom.

Religion is the master key in human study.

Knowledge without religion will breed thieves and rogues.

The first of human concerns is religion.

It is liberty which fits men for liberty.

There is another world for the expiation of guilt, but the wages of folly are payable here below.

Liberty is the essential guard of truth.

Liberty is a great and precious gift of God; human excellence cannot grow up in a nation without it.

Bustle is not business.

Constitutional freedom is a great and noble secret.

Liberty is an essential condition of excellence in human things.

As much authority as is wanted to protect the few against the many, the weak against the strong, is not contrary to freedom, but the condition of freedom. [February 19th, 1881.]

Nature is a better guide than culture, because nature comes from God and culture from man.[1]

Legislation should be for the people, and by the people; the cashiering of bad kings may be not only a right, but a duty.[2]

[1] Thomas Aquinas.
[2] Fénelon.

No war can be just unless we are compelled to it in the sole cause of freedom.

Murder may be done by legal means, by plausible and profitable war, by calumny, as well as by the dose or the dagger.

Who can tell how much we owe, in the loyalty and love of our Colonies, to the principle laid down in 1846 by Mr. Gladstone ? He was Colonial Secretary at that time, and the words were included in a speech he made at Chester. " The Colonies should be governed on the principle of freedom."

Mr. Gladstone once said : " Up to this time, men have been chosen, as a rule, for the Government, by reason of their high character, their honourable estate, birth, and upbringing, and not only for their capacity. But it remains to be proved whether men inferior in position, in birth, and education and culture, men more accustomed to the practical side of life, might not conceivably prove themselves the fittest to govern the country."

Since Christmas, 1916, often have these words come back to me. In one of Lord Acton's lectures on the French Revolution there is a passage that bears on the same idea. Dealing with the historic Declaration of the Rights of Man, at Paris, August, 1779,[1] which he describes as " a single page of print that outweighs libraries, and is stronger than all the armies of Napoleon," he adds that " it was not the work of

---

[1] " French Revolution," by Lord Acton.

superior but of mediocre minds." And Rousseau
and Tom Paine, authors of yet other trumpet calls,
were they men of education, or even of any notable
intellect ?

Lord Acton, with his vast knowledge and profound thinking, was aware that equality in this
world's goods is no more possible than equality
in the goods of any world.   Mr. Gladstone enchanted Mr. Ruskin when he pronounced himself an
" inequalitarian."   For both of them, in their wisdom,
knew that you might as well expect, by a rigid appli-
cation of Eugenics, to make all men of the same
stature and colour, of the same strength, physical or
mental or moral, of the same capacity and character,
as make all men equal simply by giving them all the
same amount of money.   If by one stroke of the
magic wand all men to-morrow were to wake up
each possessed of two hundred a year, in one week,
possibly in one day, their equality would be gone.
The Parable of the Talents is true to whatever kind
of talent it is applied—money, birth, brain, any
quality of the heart, mind or body.   Both Lord
Acton and Mr. Gladstone knew that the so-called
doctrine of equality was disastrous to the cause of
liberty.   Division of power, co-operation, brother-
hood ; the changed heart ; Christianity, in short, as
taught by its Divine Founder, with its love and its
liberty. *Cui servire, regnare est.*

I remember my feeling of pride when Lord Acton wrote down for his History two passages about Liberty that I had happened to quote to him. " *La Liberté c'est le remède de tous les maux* "—words that Ricasoli uttered in a memorable conversation with Mr. Gladstone. The other :—

> " Let there be light," said Liberty,
> And, like sunrise from the sea
> Athens arose.[1]

I must not forget an occasion at Hawarden when two undergraduates,[2] reading up their History periods, the one for the Oxford, the other for the Cambridge school, consulted Lord Acton, each on his own period ; each, to his amazement, discovered in Lord Acton a familiarity with his own period far closer than his own.

Professor Henry Sidgwick said that, however carefully and thoroughly you had mastered your special subject or period, " Acton was certain to know more."

It is interesting to compare the effect of the two speakers on their hearers, for there is much similitude in what gave both men their power and charm.

One who was present at Lord Acton's Cambridge Lectures thus describes his own sensations : " There was a magnetic quality in his voice, a light in his eye

---

[1] Shelley's " Hellas."
[2] Herbert Gladstone and Alfred Lyttelton.

that compelled obedience from the mind. Never before had a young man come into the presence of such intensity of conviction as was shown by every word Lord Acton spoke. It took possession of the whole being and seemed to enfold it in its own flame. More than all else it was this conviction that gave to his lectures their amazing force and vivacity."

While of Mr. Gladstone's speaking it has been said that every one who listened to him was equally inspired by his energy, sympathy, enthusiasm, and conviction, and found himself possessed with the same lofty emotion as himself.

In each case none could fail to see how the speaker's mind was absorbed in " the greatness of human affairs, with the final supremacy of the soul over circumstances, and the real ground for asserting the sacredness of truth and the inalienable glory of liberty." [1]

The union of faith with knowledge and the eternal supremacy of righteousness was the message delivered by both these men to mankind.

" Opinions alter, manners change, creeds rise and fall, but the moral law is inscribed on the tablets of eternity." [2]

When Mr. Gladstone had passed his eightieth year, and the General Election of 1892 had made

[1] Dr. J. Neville Figgis.
[2] J. A. Froude.

him Prime Minister for the fourth time, " I thank God," Lord Acton wrote, " now that the earthly crown of your glorious life is very near." The crown that was then in his mind was the gift of liberty to the Irish Nation.

Mr. Gladstone loved liberty, not as a policy, but for itself, and in that name he had the world for an audience. His optimism and his profound belief in his cause must have partly arisen from his conscious- ness that he was listening to the Spirit of the Age ; as has been finely expressed,[1] he was defining the thought that was to determine the future of Europe. Some day, perhaps, history may be written on these lines, the instinct of liberty as its central motive. Treaties, campaigns, the rise and fall of dynasties, of Govern- ments, of kings, as mere accidents and simply " as part of the struggle towards a fuller realisation of liberty as the spinal cord of the nation's life."

" This is what binds our history together from age to age, and gives it unity and sequence." [1]

Errors of judgment are common to all men, and Mr. Gladstone was human. But, as he once said, towards the end of his life, to Lord Morley, it was the ever-growing love of liberty that explained every apparent change, every development of his mind.

Great as was his long life of achievement, greatest of all was the man himself.

[1] L. March Phillipps.

It was about the year 1886 that John Morley first made acquaintance with Lord Acton.[1] " Friendship," he wrote, " is a relation that has many types. On none did I presume to set a more special value than on my intercourse with this observant, powerful, reflective, marvellously full mind. He saw both past history and modern politics as a whole. He was a profound master of all the lights and shades of ecclesiastical system ; a passionately interested master of the bonds between moral truth and the action of political system ; an eager explorer of the ideas that help to govern the rise and fall of States ; and a scrupulous student of the march of fact, circumstance and personality in which such ideas worked themselves through. He was comprehensive as an encyclopædia, but profound and rich, not tabulated and dry. He was a man who even on one's busiest day could seldom come amiss, so deep and unexpected was he in thought, so impressive without empty pomp of words, so copious, exact and ready in his knowledge. Once, after a great political gathering in a country town, owing to some accident of missing carriages, he and I had to walk home three or four miles along a moonlit road. I mentioned that I had engaged to make a discourse at Edinburgh on Aphorisms. This fired him, and I was speedily and most joyfully on the scent of a

[1] Lord Morley's Recollections.

whole band of German, French, Italian, and Spanish names, ample enough to carry me through half a score discourses. I never had a shorter walk. He was fond of society, but had a talent for silence that was sometimes provoking. You tempted a friend to meet him at table, and raised one hopeful topic after another; but the oracle proved dumb, and devoted himself steadily to a mute journey through the courses."

Somewhere about the year 1890, through financial stress, Lord Acton found himself compelled to place the great library he had collected at Aldenham for sale in the public market. This astonishing mass of books, collected and selected by one man, read and remembered and cherished by its creator, was to be torn away from its home, from its owner.

Mr. Gladstone took this tragedy deeply to heart, and it led him to suggest to a friend, possessed of vast wealth and corresponding generosity, to become its possessor, while it was to remain at Aldenham during the life of its creator. Mr. Carnegie was the purchaser, and only on the death of Lord Acton did he hand this great collection over to Mr. Morley.

For some days Mr. Morley played with the idea of retaining this wonderful gift. In his Recollections he tells the following story of how he handed this library of Lord Acton to the University of Cambridge.

The library has none of the treasures that are the glory of Chatsworth.   Nor is it one of those noble and miscellaneous accumulations that have been gathered by the chances of time and taste in colleges and other places of old foundation. It was collected by Lord Acton to be the material for a history of liberty, the emancipation of conscience from power, and the gradual substitution of freedom for force in the government of men.   That guiding object gives to these sixty or seventy thousand volumes a unity that I would fain preserve by placing them where they can be kept intact and in some degree apart. . . .

In this way I believe Cambridge will have the most appropriate monument of a man whom, though she thrice refused him as a learner, she afterwards welcomed as a teacher—one of the most remarkable men of our time, extraordinary in his acquisitions, extraordinary in the depth and compass of his mind.   The books will, in the opinion of scholars more competent to judge than I, be a valuable instrument of knowledge ;   but that is hardly all.   The very sight of this vast and ordered array in all departments, tongues and times, of the history of civilised governments, the growth of faiths and institutions, the fluctuating movements of human thought, all the struggles of churches and creeds, the divers types of great civil and ecclesiastical governors, the diverse ideals of States—all this will be to the ardent scholar a powerful stimulus to thought.   And it was Acton himself who said that the gifts of historical thinking are better than historical learning.   His books are sure to inspire both, for, multitudinous though they be, they concentrate the cardinal problems of modern history.

. . . I shall not forget the feeling—as on the breaking forth of some unexpected vision of the sea—with which I was taken from an upper gallery (at Aldenham) and looked upon the noble hall that contained his books, now mine, and beheld the seat and table where he had so sedulously read and ruminated and made his diligent sheaves of transcript from the silent masters around him.

It is, indeed, too true that—

no man of first-rate powers has in our time left so little by which posterity may judge those powers. Yet, if I may for an instant associate myself with posterity, I undertake, in the four volumes of lectures and essays collected by the pious zeal of his Cambridge pupils, to find at the very least one pregnant, pithy, luminous, suggestive saying in any one of their pages.

Now that we have read the Morley judgment on Lord Acton, we will turn to posterity's judgment on Mr. Gladstone, as interpreted by Lord Acton.

In September, 1879, as already mentioned, we were staying with Lord and Lady Acton at Tegernsee. One day my brother and I had rowed the three great men across the lake—Dr. Döllinger, Mr. Gladstone, and Lord Acton. Walking home with the latter, we were, in spite of an accompaniment of thunder, lightning and rain, discussing Mr. Gladstone, and I wondered what would be the judgment of posterity if, in a hundred years' time, we could come back to the earth. It was then that Lord Acton unburdened himself of the imperishable tribute which he afterwards embodied in a letter, " possibly, after the immortal funeral oration of Pericles, the noblest eulogy in existence."

The generation you consult will be democratic and better instructed than our own ; for the progress of democracy, though not constant, is certain, and the progress of knowledge is both constant and certain. It will be more severe in literary judgments and more generous in political. With this prospect before me, I ought to have answered that hereafter, when our descendants shall stand before the slab that is not yet laid among the monuments of famous Englishmen, they will say that Chatham knew how to inspire a nation with his energy, but was poorly furnished with knowledge and ideas ; that the capacity of Fox was never proved in office, though he was the first of debaters ; that Pitt, the strongest of ministers, was among the weakest of legislators ; that no Foreign Secretary has equalled Canning, but that he showed no other administrative ability ; that Peel, who excelled as an adminis- trator, a debater, and a tactician, fell everywhere short of genius ; and that the highest merits of the five, without their drawbacks, were united in Mr. Gladstone. Possibly they may remember that his only rival in depth and wealth and force of mind was neither admitted to the Cabinet nor buried in the Abbey. They will not say of him, as of Burke, that his writing equalled his speaking, or surpassed it, like Macaulay's. For though his books manifest the range of his powers, if they do not establish a distinct and substantive reputation, they will breed regret that he suffered anything to divert him from that career in which his supremacy was undisputed among the men of his time. People who suspect that he sometimes disparaged himself by not recognising the secret of his own superiority will incline to believe that he fell into another error of wise and good men, who are not ashamed to fail in the rigid estimate of characters and talents. This will serve them to explain his lofty unfitness to deal with sordid motives, and to control that undignified but necessary work ; his inability to sway certain kinds of men, and that strange property of his influence, which is greatest with multitudes, less in society—and least at home.   And it will help them to understand a mystery that is becoming very prominent—that he formed no school and left no disciples who were to him what Windham, Grenville, Wellesley, Canning, Castlereagh, were to Pitt ; that his colleagues followed him because he had the nation at his back, by force more than by persuasion, and chafed, as he did by the side of Palmerston.

Some keys, I imagine, will be lost, and some finer lines will yield to the effacing fingers. . . .

But all the things about which no New Zealander will feel as we do, do not disturb your appeal to the serene and impartial judgment of history.   When our problems are solved and our struggles ended, when distance has restored the proportions of things, and the sun has set for all but the highest summits, his fame will increase even in things where it seems impossible to add to it.   Ask all the clever men you know, who were the greatest British orators, and there are ten or twelve names that will appear on every list.   There is no such acknowledged primacy among them as Mirabeau enjoys in France or Webster in America.   Macaulay told me that Brougham was the best speaker he had heard ; Lord Russell preferred Plunket ; and Gaskell, Canning.   I have heard people who judged by efficacy assign the first place to Peel, O'Connell, Palmerston. . . .

But the illustrious chain of English eloquence that begins in the Walpolean battles ends with Mr. Gladstone.   His rivals divide his gifts, like the generals of Alexander.   One

may equal him in beauty of composition, another in the art
of statement, and a third perhaps comes near him in fluency
and fire.   But he alone possesses all the qualities of an orator ;
and when men come to remember what his speeches accomplished, how it was the same whether he prepared an oration
or hurled a reply, whether he addressed a British mob or the
cream of Italian politicians, and would still be the same if he
spoke in Latin to Convocation, they will admit no rival.

" *C'est la grandeur de Berryer avec la souplesse de Thiers,*"
was the judgment of the ablest of the Ultramontanes [1] on his
speech on Charities.

There are especially two qualities which will not be found
in other men : First, the vigorous and perpetual progress of
his mind.

Later ages will know what in this critical autumn of a
famous year [2] is only guessed, that even now, at 70, in his
second ministry, after half a century of public life, his
thoughts are clearing, moving, changing, on the two highest
of all political questions.

His other pre-eminent characteristic is the union of
theory and policy. . . . In Mr. Gladstone there is all the
resource and policy of the heroes of Carlyle's worship, and
yet he moves scrupulously along the lines of the science of
statesmanship.   Those who deem that Burke was the first
political genius until now must at this point admit his
inferiority. He loved to evade the arbitration of principle.
He was prolific of arguments that were admirable, but not
decisive.   He dreaded two-edged weapons and maxims that
faced both ways. . . .

Looking abroad, beyond the walls of Westminster, for
objects worthy of comparison, they will say that other men,

[1] Montalembert.
[2] December, 1880.

such as Hamilton and Cavour, accomplished work as great ;
that Turgot and Roon were unsurpassed in administrative
craft ; that Clay and Thiers were as dexterous in Parliamen-
tary management ; that Berryer and Webster resembled him
in gifts of speech, Guizot and Radowitz in fulness of thought ;
but that in the three elements of greatness combined—the
man, the power, and the result—character, genius, and
success—none reached his level.

The decisive test of his greatness will be the gap he will
leave.   Among those who come after him there will be none
who understand that the men who pay wages ought not to be
the political masters of those who earn them (because laws
should be adapted to those who have the heaviest stake in the
country, for whom misgovernment means not mortified pride
or stinted luxury, but want and pain and degradation, and
risk to their own lives and to their children's souls), and
who yet can understand and feel sympathy for institutions
that incorporate tradition and prolong the reign of the dead.

Fill the blanks, deepen the contrasts, shut your ears to the
tones of my voice, and if you make believe very much, you
shall hear the roll of the ages.[1]

Mr. Gladstone was buried (1898) in the great Abbey
which is the most precious monument of our history.

Lord Morley's unforgettable description of the
mourning nations around his death-bed—France,
America, Russia, Italy, Greece, Roumania, Monte-
negro, Norway, Denmark, and the Balkan races—
nations that had struggled, or were still struggling,
to be free—concludes with these words : " It was

---

[1] Lord Acton's Letters.

not at Westminster only that his praise went forth ;
famous men have the whole world for their tomb ;
in foreign lands a memorial of them is graven in the
hearts of men. No other statesman on our famous
roll has touched the imagination of so wide a world."

Lord Acton was laid to rest in the quiet churchyard at Tegernsee, near the cherished little daughter
whose death-bed he had comforted with the words :
" Be glad, my child, you will soon be with Jesus
Christ."

To both of these men centuries of errors, heavily
burdened with sin and suffering, had not disturbed
their faith in the promise of Christianity. They
both " wooed religion with the unflinching sincerity
of love, grateful for the graces which from the
cradle to the grave had been vouchsafed to them.
They committed the future of Catholic Christendom
—and with it of mankind itself—to the paternal love
and care of One who is patient because He is eternal,
of One to whom a thousand years is as one day." [1]

> Let us praise famous men,
>   Men of little showing—
> For their word continueth,
> Deep and long continueth,
> Wide and far continueth,
>   Far beyond their knowing.[2]

[1] " Quarterly Review."
[2] Rudyard Kipling.

CHAPTER II

MR. GLADSTONE'S BOOKS

" Whose service is perfect freedom."

"HOW was this library built, and what is it for ?"
This question was asked in the autumn of
1905 by a distinguished member of the House of
Lords, a prominent Churchman, and a relation,
moreover, of one of the St. Deiniol's trustees. If the
educated world is still in such darkness as this query
implies, of the aim and purpose of a library collected
by Mr. Gladstone, presented by him to the students
of Great Britain, and of a building erected by the
Nation in his memory, it is certainly time that some
authoritative account should be supplied. I am glad
of the opportunity to supply as best I can this need.
To begin with his own words :

Convinced that the future of the human race depends, in
the main, upon the great question of belief, and that the most
special and urgent of present needs is the need of sufficient
means for the effective promotion of Divine learning, I am
engaged in the foundation of a Library, which I trust may
serve as the nucleus of an Institution, under the name of St.
Deiniol's, Hawarden, adapted to that end. Divine learning,
in order to reach its fullest efficiency, has been and ought to

be associated with the various branches of human knowledge, especially with History and Philosophy ; and it is upon the widest basis that the Library is being formed. The religious *intuitus* of the Institution will be conformity to the living spirit of the Church of England ; which I am persuaded will do nothing in regard to faith and discipline to compromise or impair her character as the Catholic and Apostolic Church of this country. Wholly dependent upon voluntary alms, the Institution will have no concern with any question relating to the temporalities or civil status of the Church. Such an endowment as I contemplate providing for it, or as it may hereafter receive from any source, will be placed in the hands of a Trust which I now desire to constitute, and which will be the governing body of the Institution.

With that main design—the effective promotion of Divine learning—there will, I hope, be associated other secondary but harmonising purposes, one of which is now and has for more than a year and a half been in actual operation. While the principles of the Institution will be those of the historic Church of this country, and while the Governing Body will be appointed to work upon that idea, it is my earnest desire and full intention that the hospitality of the Institution and its conveniences and advantages should as far as possible be made available for persons beyond the pale of the Anglican Church or even of the Christian Religion. There would be an honourable obligation on their side to use the opportunities afforded them, not for purposes merely secular, but for religious obligation or service, and to respect in spirit as well as in letter the rules and usages of the place ; with a corresponding obligation on the other side to uphold their personal religious liberty in the amplest sense, and to require of them nothing at variance with the rights of conscience.

These words appear in the preliminary paper drawn up in October, 1895, by Mr. Gladstone with a view to the formation of the Trust. They will remind the reader of another writer, also renowned for his learning, who held that " religion was the master-key in human study."

We all know [he wrote] some twenty or thirty predominant currents of thought . . . or system bearing principles, which weave the web of human history and constitute the civilised opinion of the age. All these, I imagine, a serious man ought to understand in whatever strength or weakness they possess, in their causes or effects, and in their relation to each other. The majority of them are religious, or substitutes for religion. . . . All understanding of history depends on one's understanding the forces that make it, and religious forces are the most active and the most definite. To develop and perfect and arm conscience is the great achievement of history, the chief business of every life—and the first agent therein is religion.[1]

Here is the great principle that underlay the relations between these two men—the keynote of their friendship. " Religion is the master-key in the study of life," " the great question of belief in the main the first concern of the human race," expressions surely of profound significance, as coming not from ecclesiastical lips, but as the deliberately expressed conviction of two of the greatest and most learned laymen of the nineteenth century. And the

[1] " Lord Acton's Letters."

living witness of their faith is to be seen in the libraries collected by the two men—St. Deiniol's Library at Hawarden, and the Acton Library at Cambridge.

Mr. Gladstone was a lover of books from a very early period. From his own record we know that two of the books that took the strongest hold on him as a child were " The Pilgrim's Progress " and " The Arabian Nights," and his mother has related how he used to lie on the floor devouring Froissart's " Chronicles " at a fabulously early age. In a glass case at St. Deiniol's Library are preserved specimens of his Eton schoolbooks, his autograph signature even at that time characteristic of his handwriting in later years. The notes in these boy-books are copious— headings, diagrams, neat annotations, mathematical problems. The blank interleaving pages of the " Cicero " are illustrated with the miscellaneous scribblings and drawings usual with schoolboys, and in the " Iliad " one of the leaves is adorned with the plan of a cricket match (let us recall that he was in the Eton twenty-two), the names of the players, and their places in the field. From the sketch of the cricket-field scribbled in his early " Homer," the visitor will be interested to move on and examine a later edition of the poet in three octavo volumes, in which nearly seventy years later Mr. Gladstone read the " Iliad " for the thirtieth time, finding it at every

reading " richer and more glorious than before."
(In reading the " Odyssey " he always used the same
one-volume edition, having it rebound whenever it
wore out with constant handling.) " Ever since," he
wrote, " I began to pass out of boyhood, I have been
feeling my way, owing little to living teachers, but
enormously to four dead ones, over and above the
Four Gospels." This Mr. Gladstone wrote at the
age of sixty-nine, the four to whom he referred being,
as is well known, Aristotle, Augustine, Dante, and
Butler.

The following incident is here related, as, though
unimportant in itself, it illustrates how little Mr.
Gladstone ever realised his position in the hearts
and minds of mankind, and the interest that might
belong to relics connected with his youth. A quarto
MS. book bound in red leather, in a state of excellent
preservation, bore the dates, in his own boyish handwriting, 1819 (when he was nine, at Eton) and 1828
(when he was eighteen, at Christ Church). This
book he one day accidentally lit upon. Six or eight
pages were covered with beautifully written mathematical notes and diagrams. These he neatly cut
out, and, presenting the book to a member of his
family, expressed a hope that now he had removed
the offending pages, it might be of some service.
One page of diagrams in the middle of the volume
had luckily escaped his notice, and for this and the

early autograph signatures the book is treasured in a manner very contrary to his anticipations.

Somewhere about the year 1860 the housing of his growing library necessitated the addition of a new wing to the Castle at Hawarden.   As a kind of pledge of sanctity, the " Temple of Peace " was the name chosen for the room set apart for his books. Conversation in the ordinary sense of the word— though many an important consultation and interview took place there—was strictly prohibited, but members of the family, or friends staying in the house, were at liberty to make use of the room for purposes of study or reading, and so absorbed was its owner that he was usually quite unaware of their presence.

Mr. Gladstone was by no means a rabid book-buyer.   Rare books, first editions, and elaborate bindings had no especial attraction for him, though when they came to him as gifts they were eagerly welcomed.   A book should be fitly bound ; it consists, he liked to remind his friends, like men from whom it draws its lineage, of a body and a soul. Noble works should not appear in mean and worthless dress.

Paper [he said], type, and ink are the body in which the soul is domiciled.   And these three, body, soul, and habiliment, are a triad which should be adjusted to one another by the laws of harmony and good sense.   Books are the voices of the dead—a main instrument of communion with the vast human procession of the other world.   Second to none as friends to the individual, they are first and foremost as bonds and rivets of the race.

So human and personal did a book seem to Mr. Gladstone that it gave him real pain to see it carelessly used, or illtreated—laid open on its face, untidily marked, dog's-eared, thumbed.   And in arranging his friends on the shelf, no squeezing or even coaxing was allowed ;   they must fit in with nicety, not wasting space, but in no way uncomfortably housed.

Second-hand catalogues rained in by every post, and were always carefully scanned, and marked for immediate purchase.   Subjects such as witchcraft, strange religious sects, duelling, gipsies, epitaphs, the ethics of marriage, not to mention Homer, Shakespeare, and Dante, invariably commanded an order.   Quickly the room filled ;   one by one each piece of extraneous furniture disappeared to make way for low bookcases suited to serve as tables and to hold volumes of abnormal size.   Like Browning's rats :—

came tumbling
Great books, small books, lean books, brawny books,
Brown books, black books, grey books, tawny books,
Grave old plodders, gay young friskers,
Fathers, mothers, uncles, cousins,
Families by tens and dozens.

They overflowed into the vestibule, they ran along the passage into the billiard-room ; this involved the disappearance of the billiard table. Prizes were offered for the discovery of possible new spaces for bookcases. Often pondering, as he did, how best to benefit his fellow creatures, how to bring together readers who had no books and books who had no readers, gradually the thought evolved itself in his mind into a plan for the permanent disposal of his library. A country home for the purposes of study and research, " for the pursuit of Divine learning," a centre of religious life, a resident body of students, men of studious mind and habit, unfitted by various causes for active life or the turmoil of great cities.

But so sceptical were most of those to whom he confided his plan, as to the need of such a home of learning, divorced from city life and conditions, that he resolved cautiously, tentatively to feel his way ; to run no risk of wasting money over stone or bricks and mortar, to erect a temporary iron building for the housing of his library, to furnish a temporary house for the reception of the students. In 1889 two large iron rooms, lined with felt and pine, were erected, with six or seven smaller ones to act as studies, on the crest of Hawarden Hill, and the travel of the books began. Twenty-seven thousand were carried up the hill. Any one who has himself moved a few hundred books from one room to another in the same house will appreciate the sheer hard manual labour that Mr. Gladstone put into this migration of his library from one house to another. Each book he took down from the shelves, and each packet he strapped up with his own hands, and no vehicle was ever allowed to leave the Castle without its consignment of book bundles. Arrived at their destination, they were laid upon the floor in the order in which they came, and Mr. Gladstone, unaided save by his valet and sometimes one of his daughters, when home from Cambridge, unstrapped and lifted and sifted and placed the volumes one by one in the bookcases prepared to receive them. His habits " savoured more of serious handiwork in the arrangement of a library than of lordly survey and direction." " And," he adds, " what man who really loves his books delegates to any other human being, as long as there is breath in his body, the office of introducing them into their homes ? "

The cost of a book, he pointed out, is sanguinely believed by its purchaser to be a thing completed and done with when he places his coins on the counter and receives his receipted bill. But this was a popular superstition. Such payment is not the last but the first in a series of goodly length. Assuming an ordinary purchase, the book, if worthy of prolonged life, must be bound, then it must be placed in a bookcase, the bookcase must be bought and housed, and the house must be kept, and the library must be cleaned, dusted, arranged, catalogued. Yet he considered one shilling a volume a handsome allowance for one part of the process—the housing of the books in a gentleman's library ; and acting on the principles he adopted in later life, using bookcases made of pitch pine, devoid of all carving or ornament, he ended by calculating it could be done at a penny a volume.

Often had the anxious problem come into his mind, the over-population of the world, not by people but by books, the over-pressure not on subsistence, but on space. Twenty thousand volumes were annually pouring into the Bodleian, forty thousand into the British Museum. Every year, he calculated, even at that period, nearly twenty years ago, half a mile of new shelving was required.

And whatever [he said] may be the rate of growth now, it is small in comparison with what it is likely to become. The key of the question lies in the hands of the United Kingdom and the United States. They, with their vast range of inhabited territory and their unity of tongue, are masters of the world. When Britons and Americans are fused into one book market, when artificial fetters are relaxed, and printers, publishers, and authors obtain the reward which well-regulated commerce would afford them, then let floors beware lest they crack, and walls lest they bulge and burst from the weight of books they will have to carry and to confine.

A decent burial he ventured to suggest—not cremation, but interment—for books unsuitable for daily companionship ; among these, finding in them little sociability, he would have included his " Hansards."

But at all events he was resolved, by the strictest economy of space, by placing the maximum of volumes in the minimum of room, to postpone as far as possible the evil day when the world would be choking with its over-population of books. His objects were three—economy of space, ease of accessibility, and arrangement by subject. The bookcases project at right angles from the wall ; each contains three faces, the shelves are fixed, and so accurately are their height and depth adjusted to the length and breadth of the books, that, back to back as they stand, the smallest waste of space is scarcely discernible to the minutest examination. Between the projections, unless occupied by windows, the wall spaces are also used for shallow bookshelves, so that each recess is a three-sided book-lined compartment. Fixed shelves he found most conducive to the vital purposes of compression. To begin with, they contribute to the strength and firmness of the bookcase itself, as they hold the parts together. Then it is a great matter, in addition to other advantages, to avoid the endless trouble and the misfits of movable shelves, the weight, the tightness or the looseness, the weary arms, the aching fingers, the broken finger-nails, not to mention the murderous temper and *à quoi bon?*, always to discover the books are too large for the space, or the space too large for the books. And, moreover, there is not so much variety in the sizes of books as might be imagined from a superficial acquaintance with them. Octavos now hold the field ; more and more are they considered the classical size ; the octavo, with some exceptions, is now professionally the library edition. By much careful reckoning and measurement of sizes, shapes, numbers of his books, and the proportions in which the various sizes required accommodation, Mr. Gladstone reached an accurate knowledge of their requirements. He allowed that here and there, by way of exception, a single movable shelf may be introduced to meet occasional imperfections or miscalculation in the computation of sizes.

Having now dealt with his first two objects, economy of space and ease of accessibility, we reach the third and most important—that of arrangement ; whether to distribute the books by alphabet, by author, by subject, or by size. Mr. Gladstone settled on distribution by subject. " Yet subjects," he said, " are traversed by promiscuous assemblages of works, both by sizes and by languages." For a catalogue he recommended alphabetical arrangement with well-chosen subdivisions. Among others, he pleaded for individual authors as centres of subdivision, not only for Homer, Dante, Shakespeare, but for John-

son, Scott, Burns, and whoever and whatever represented a large and manifold humanity. But in
settling for distribution by subject, he owned it must
in some degree be controlled by size. A friend suggested to him that five classes would suffice : Science,
Speculation, Art, History, and, lastly, Miscellaneous
and Periodical Literature. This apparently simple
method of classifying lands the librarian in innumerable difficulties. The bounds of Speculation are
limitless, the diversities in Science would render sub-
classification imperative.

The 'ologies are by no means well suited to rub shoulders
together, and Sciences must include Arts, which are but
country cousins to them, or a new compartment must be
established for their accommodation. And how to cope
with the everlasting difficulty of " Works " ? In what cate-
gory to place Dante, Petrarch, Swedenborg, Burke, Coleridge,
Carlyle, Macaulay, or a hundred more ? Where is Poetry
to stand ? It must take its place—the first place without
doubt—in Art, for while separated from Painting and her
other sphere-born sisters by their greater dependence on
material form, they are each and all profoundly united in
their first and all-enfolding principle—which is to organise
the beautiful for presentation to the perceptions of man.

Here he lays down one of his favourite axioms,
imbibed from Lessing. In the " Laocoon " Lessing
had, as Mr. Gladstone felt, promulgated for all time
the definition of Art—*i.e.*, the defining by analysis
the limitations of Art, and the fruitful principle that,

each art being subject to definite conditions, only by
obeying its laws and recognising its limits can the
artist, whether painter or poet, architect, musician,
or novelist, accomplish great results. Bourget has
said the same thing—it is easier to write fact than
fiction. In the former there is no limit ; nothing is
too extraordinary, too unnatural to be occasionally
true in fact. But in fiction the writer is held fast
in the bonds of the normal and the ordinary. The
author who does not wish to court failure " must
trudge humbly along the old thoroughfares where
the pavements are trodden and worn by the feet of
other pilgrims now gone to their Eternal City—that
City which no by-way ever yet reached." A sense
of harmony, of fitness, in literature as in other
matters, is one of the rarest of Heaven's gifts. This
was the secret of Mr. Gladstone's boundless enjoy-
ment of Walter Scott : the presentation to mankind
of, not the ugly, the unnatural, the cruel, the base,
but the lofty, the beautiful, the ideal. Now and then
he would find a novel of our own day that fulfilled his
sense of harmony. " The Minister's Wooing," by
Mrs. Stowe, is one of these ; " John Inglesant " is
another. But this is a digression, and we must not
be drawn by the fascination of the subject from the
main purpose of this review.

Enough has been said to make clear Mr. Gladstone's principles in the arrangement of his library.

We have touched on his main design as to its use. In the old temporary structure he had stored nearly 30,000 volumes, divided, roughly, into two sections —Humanity and Divinity :

> The negative movement of the age [he wrote] aims at establishing a severance between the Christian system and the general thought of the time ; its history, philosophy, physical science, poetry and literature at large. But no enlightened Christian will admit that our Christianity was intended to be an isolated thing, standing apart from all other conditions of our life. The comprehensiveness of Creation and of human nature are a perpetual lesson to us, teaching that we should aim at nothing narrower than a Christianity which is to cover the whole ground of our complete existence. This is our charter : and we cannot consent to its multilation or contraction. We assert the right of the Gospel to associate with every just influence over the whole sphere of our nature and its functions. In the right cultivation and retention of them all, God is to be glorified.

To " improve and maybe perfect our means of maintaining the harmony between Christian knowledge and all other knowledge " was his aim. " The especial purpose that I have in view is this sacred marriage, so to call it, between the grand process ordained for the recovery of our nature from sin, and its healthy general development." This passage illumines the two words—Humanity and Divinity.

In 1894 the first students took up their temporary abode in the adjoining house, and the first Warden selected by Mr. Gladstone was the son-in-law[1] who lived under his roof. In this happy and harmonious arrangement there was the signal advantage of constant and intimate intercourse and consultation ; the best opportunity of imbibing from the founder his ideas, hopes, and aspirations for the development of this " home of learning." The most important work started and completed by Mr. Drew was the Catalogue, which it took him two years to complete. It was made on the card system, and is a cross catalogue, each book being at least twice inscribed, by its author and by its subject. So long as the buildings were temporary, the secondary purposes of the Institution could be fulfilled—viz., " to provide retirement with means of study for persons, especially clergy, employed, and desiring temporary rest." These objects, secondary and auxiliary, as Mr. Gladstone describes them in his trust deed, so far, then, have been gained. But the main purposes have also been partially fulfilled by the resident Wardens.

In 1898, on the death of the founder, the Committee formed for the National Memorial came to the conclusion that part of the money subscribed could hardly be more appropriately spent than in the erection of a permanent building to hold Mr. Gladstone's books. The sum of £10,000 was offered to the Trustees and accepted by them. In 1899 Mrs.

[1] The Rev. Harry Drew.

Gladstone cut the first sod, and the Duke of Westminster, on behalf of the National Memorial Committee, laid the first stone of the Library. The service of dedication was read by the Bishop of St.
Asaph, in the presence of Mrs. Gladstone and her
family, the Rector of Hawarden, chairman of the
Trustees, and other friends and neighbours. The
foundation-stone, which is of green granite, on the
southern side of the Library, bears this inscription :
" In this building, erected to his memory by a grateful nation, is preserved the library of WILLIAM
EWART GLADSTONE, who, eminent no less as a
theologian than as a statesman, established this
foundation for the advancement of Divine learning. This stone was laid in the presence of the
Lord Bishop of the Diocese by the Duke of
Westminster, K.G., Oct. 5, 1899. G. C. JOYCE,
Warden."

On the 14th of October, 1902, St. Deiniol's
Library was formally opened. It is a striking edifice
in a striking situation, and forms, with the ancient
church in the background, a group of buildings that
cannot fail to arrest the eyes of passers-by. Built of
red sandstone, its internal arrangements are harmonious for its purpose. Two halls, with galleries
above supported by pillars, form the main feature.
The woodwork is all oak. Semi-privacy is obtained
here in the nooks formed by the bookcases, and there

are besides other private rooms for the students.[1] In Lord Spencer's inaugural speech comment was made on the inadequacy of the sum set aside for the yearly purchase of books, and he observed that forty times the amount then spent was laid out on the Althorp Library now at Manchester. " But I am confident," he added, " that when this work is known, the largeness of its aims, the spirit of toleration with which it is marked, assistance will come which will carry out the work in a manner worthy of the name with which it is associated." Gaps there undoubtedly are, and contributions to the Library would be of great value. Three hundred pounds a year was the sum suggested by the founder as a minimum. For this purpose, and for the maintenance of the institution as a whole, he endowed it with £30,000. Roughly speaking, £60,000 has been devoted to the scheme—£40,000 by Mr. Gladstone himself, £10,000 by the nation for housing the books, and the remainder by his sons and daughters for housing the men ; the latter constituting their joint memorial to their father.

In 1904 Mr. Gladstone's family undertook the task of completing the group of buildings, by erecting a permanent residence for the staff and for the students. As to the methods of fulfilling that design

[1] Any one wishing for either temporary or more permanent residence should apply to the Warden, St. Deiniol's Library, Hawarden, who would supply all information as to the very moderate terms, regulations and privileges, etc.

A. E

jointly or severally—whether in training men for
Holy Orders, or affiliating itself to some community
already in working order, or whether by a resident
body of men, studying, learning, working for
Christianity by writings, or by active participation
in the ministrations of the Church, or by courses of
lectures and instructions in different parts of Wales
—Mr. Gladstone, while contemplating these several
methods of attaining his purpose, left the choice open
to the trustees, always provided it be " deliberately
judged by them to be required for the better fulfil-
ment of the main design."

Lord Spencer, when opening St. Deiniol's Library
in 1902, referred, in terms of reverent admiration, to
the example Mr. Gladstone set in uniting the spirit
of toleration for the principles of others with his own
deep spiritual convictions, and specially in not desiring to limit the benefits of the Library to men of his
own creed. " It is true," said Lord Spencer, " it
was his pious hope that neither the buildings nor the
books should be used for purposes hostile to the
Church." Mr. Gladstone realised, as do all who
possess definite religious convictions, that there can
be no more vital mistake than to try to water down
the historic Church of England to suit the susceptibilities of those who hold different views, to make her
into a huge jelly-fish without form and void, giving
way to pressure from each and every side in turn.

The love of freedom, which in Mr. Gladstone amounted to a passion, was deeply rooted in his belief in law and discipline. " Freedom is the flower of slavery," as has been finely said in our own day.

To a member of the Unitarian body, Mr. Gladstone wrote in 1865 :—

I am, as you know, one altogether attached to dogma, which I believe to be the skeleton that carries the flesh, the blood, the life of the blessed thing we call the Christian religion. But I do not believe God's tender mercies are restricted to a small portion of the human family. . . . I was myself brought up to believe that salvation depended absolutely on the reception of a particular and very narrow creed. But long, long have I cast those weeds behind me.

" Tolerance," says Mr. Morley in commenting on this declaration, " means reverence for all the possibilities of truth ; it means acknowledgment that she dwells in diverse mansions and wears vestures of many colours and speaks in strange tongues . . . it means the charity that is even greater than faith and hope." [1]

A distinguished Nonconformist, speaking on behalf of his brethren at the opening of the Library, said that though " he represented a branch of the great Christian family to which Mr. Gladstone did not belong, there was no man who had so little sympathy

---

[1] Morley's " Life of Gladstone," Vol. II., pp. 136, 137.

E 2

with Nonconformist opinions who yet appealed more
strongly to the Nonconformist heart. When the
question of voting a grant to St. Deiniol's Library
came before the Gladstone Memorial Committee,
there were some members [he said] who feared that
the Nonconformist section might be staggered by
the idea of a purely Anglican institution being assisted
out of that particular fund. But," continued Dr.
Guinness Rogers, himself a member of the Memorial
Committee, " you don't understand Nonconformists.
We don't object to sympathise with men in their own
opinions and beliefs. . . . It was the men who
fought most strongly for their own conscience who
were most ready to respect the consciences of
others."

" It is my earnest desire," wrote the founder, " that
the hospitality of the Institution should be as far as
possible available for persons beyond the pale of the
Anglican Church." Not a school, not a college or a
free library, in the ordinary sense, but a home for
mental and spiritual refreshment and research, open
to thinkers of every class, even to those to whom
the gift of faith has been denied, earnest inquirers,
seekers, searchers after the truth that is divine. A
spirit of reverence, a love of truth, sympathy with
the aims of the founder, this is all that is demanded
of its students and visitors. The founder hoped that
the Library " would not be used for purposes

hostile to the Church of England." This is expressed in the trust deed. But for " the advancement of divine learning " he looked specially to the resident community. And the type of men that undoubtedly he had in view, and to whom he in the first instance offered the wardenship, were men residing and working in religious communities already existing and in working order, men who by the example of their lives and the fruits of their labours, by their learning, their teaching, their writings and their ministrations, would form at Hawarden a living centre of religion, and would do for their own generation what Pusey and Stubbs, Lightfoot and Westcott had done for theirs. Mr. Gladstone saw that in an age when the negative tendencies of thought were seeking to dethrone Christianity from its true predominance over the intellectual and moral development of humanity, it would be good to revive something of the methods of the wise of old. By their lives that predominance had originally been won, by their austere experience they had shown it could best be sustained by the spiritual discipline of the consecrated life, inspired and strengthened by corporate devotion and aspiration. In the words of the greatest Christian philosopher [1] of our own day—a writer who pleads for

---

[1] J. R. Illingworth, "Bampton Lecturer," author of " Divine Immanence," " Reason and Revelation," " Christian Character," &c., died August, 1915.

some such recovery of the ancient spirit in dealing with our own moral problems—" And this lesson we need not scorn to learn from what larger minds in calmer ages thought out with prayer and fasting, we whose minds are weaker and whose lives unquiet, and who seldom fast or pray."

CHAPTER III

HENRY SCOTT HOLLAND

PART I

> . . . in such hour of need . . .
> Ye like angels appear,
> Radiant with ardour divine . . .
> Langour is not in your heart,
> Weakness is not in your word,
> Weariness not on your brow . . .
> Ye fill up the gaps in our files,
> Strengthen the wavering line,
> Stablish, continue our march,
> On to the bound of the waste,
> On to the City of God.

HIS was an arresting personality. No one could be in the same room with him for five minutes and be unconscious of the presence of a kindling force, a compelling fire, some quality absolutely different to everything and everybody else. One of our public men has spoken of him as a " flaming vitality, so alive as to give to most of those around him an appearance of intellectual torpor. It was as a sword, a fire, a challenge that he appeared to us." Yet the very utmost that can be said or written, besides conveying a possible sense of exaggeration, must fail to give to those who never came within the magic of his presence any accurate conception of its influence. The truth is there are no words in the English language too superlative—his friends forget all measure and restraint when they try to describe what he was to them. They despair of conveying any idea of what he was, so alive, so near, so real and even tangible a presence he remains for us. Death cannot rob us of him—the word seems meaningless when applied to his vivid personality, to his unquestioned presence. For myself I have not even attempted to realise that he is gone. Nothing that ever happened to me, no event public or private, no new book I had read, no new friend I had made, was ever complete until it had been shared with him, and most of his friends would say the same. In his study at Oxford, in the garden that he loved at Christ Church, even at Amen Court, I see him, I hear his voice, I feel his nearness.

Light is the element with which our beloved friend is inseparably associated. His nature had all the attributes of light—its revealing power, its cheerfulness, its salubrity, its transforming beauty, its inconceivable rapidity. He saw with a flash into the heart of an argument or a situation. He diffused joy by his own joy in living—he vanquished morbidity by his essential wholesomeness." [1]

He dispelled darkness in his own light, he conquered doubt by the fire of his faith—like a swift

[1] G. W. E. Russell.

river cleansing every blade of glass, every crumb of clay with which it came in contact, like a flame that transforms, annihilating evil, like a sea breeze quickening, bracing, sweeping out the dusty corners of the soul, renewing life and love. He set us thinking. He kept us going. He lifted life to a new level. " He was not the Light : but he came to bear witness of the Light "—and grandly he bore it for seventy years by the mere force of what he was.

As Bishop Francis Paget said of him, " He is so high, yet so easy to get at : his whole life is a rendering of Christianity into language that we can understand—the language of daily normal work and rest, raising and ennobling just as the Bible ennobles the common English."

Some of us enjoy giving special names to our friends. For Ruskin it was " Aprile "—Browning's description in " Paracelsus " being a living picture of him. Burne Jones was " Angelo." At Eton H. S. H. bore the nickname of " Monkey " or " *Linky Holland.*" (" The Link " he was named by W. Johnson.) My name for him was the " Flying Dutchman " or the " *Fliegende Holländer.*" He was in some sense associated with wings.

As one of his dearest friends said—there is this especial difficulty about getting any one who did not know him to realise what he was. Generally one can say in describing any one, he was something like so and so, he reminded me of this or that conspicuous figure, X, Y or Z. So one tries to describe or explain through comparison with others. There may, indeed, be some superficial resemblance to him in this or that man, *e.g.*, in some ardent disciple, but in every case it is Holland trimmed and stripped of all that touched the skies. He belonged to no school. Generally this signifies a colourless nature, but with him nothing can be further from the truth. His character was his own : his thoughts were his own, they never reflected those of other men. He was conspicuously original. Yet there was no effort to be original, nor even a consciousness that he was so. It was this that made him so intensely interesting. Not Jowett or Green, Westcott or Liddon influenced his opinions. Much as he owed to T. H. Green, it was his intellect not his character that was influenced. Green taught him how to look at things, how to look at life, how to look at phenomena or things seen, on to the spiritual principles they embody or shadow forth. Dr. King [1] he most specially loved and revered, because of the moral beauty of his character. Undoubtedly independence of thought was a marked characteristic of his mind.

One [2] only comes to my mind as I think of him, a swift and passing vision, as he himself describes her,

[1] Bishop of Lincoln.
[2] Laura Tennant, married Alfred Lyttelton, May, 1885 ; died April, 1886.

for she died when she was twenty-three, and it is impossible to tell into what flower this entrancing bud would have blossomed. But there can be no doubt she had the same irresistible charm, the same irrepressible fun. The likeness between them lay in their vitality, in their lightning understanding and power of putting themselves into the place of others, in their glorious sense of the ridiculous, which more than all things signifies true sense of proportion, in the brilliant quality of their brains, the breadth and depth of their sympathies, the purity and selflessness and aspiration of their religion. To be nearer to God was the consuming passion of their lives, the fire of God was in their hearts.

This similarity was apparent the moment they met—the effect was electric, the meeting of two rockets. First and foremost among their gifts was the gift of vision—they saw straight through the flesh to the spirit : they contrived to set on fire anything that lay smouldering within, they quickened with their own flame all whom they met. Everything that they touched they vitalised, their own brilliancy they contrived to impart to others. No one could be dull in their presence. The most uninteresting person would suddenly find him or her self invested with an unsuspected power, an undreamed-of charm ; the dull became witty, the slow found themselves quick, the mean became generous. Above everything

they were keen and stimulating listeners, far more
keen to hear than to speak, more anxious to draw out
the experiences of others than to impart their own.
How well I remember a dinner party when, unfor-
tunately, the talk fell on a topic of rather mundane
human experience [1]—it was a subject that would
appeal to the dreariest people ; while rebelling at the
waste of time, in one way it was interesting to me,
for it was that evening I realised one secret of his
charm. There was not a person seated round the
table (except Dr. Holland) but was dying to tell his
or her own experience. He alone never capped the
experience of others with his own. It was they who
described, he who asked and listened.

Did any man ever bring so vivid a sense of the
supremacy of mind over matter as Dr. Holland ?
Though in his earlier days well-knit and slight of
build, conspicuous for alertness, agility and grace of
movement, tall and slender and vital, it was still the
over-mastering realisation of the indwelling spirit
that captured. As he grew older it mattered little to
us that he had lost the perfect proportions of his
physical presence and symmetry, so strong was the
sense of his soul. There is an evening at Hawarden
that lives in the memory of those who were present.
He was addressing a group of fine young gymnasts.
He had watched their performance with eager

[1] Sea-sickness.

delight, the beautiful action, the turns and twists, the prowess and poise of their youthful bodies appealed to his sense of beauty, the sense of mastery kindled his enthusiasm. And then he talked to them. In all the thrill of his delight it was of the spirit that he spoke so earnestly. He kindled their imagination ; he made them realise, as they listened, that the outward and visible sign was as nothing in comparison with the inward and spiritual grace. So vividly did he speak of the indwelling soul, that suddenly he felt the need of reminding them once again of that hampering though splendid thing, the body—the body with its temptations, its impurities, its appetites, its gorgeous possibilities. " After all has been said and done," he said, " we must remember that we all of us, *or very nearly all of us*, are accompanied by a body." And those who heard him, " *very nearly all of us*," suddenly felt the conviction that here was the exception—the man who was speaking unconsciously describing himself—it was he whose spirit was so permeating and transmuting that the body did not count. One or two who were present arrived home literally intoxicated with what they had heard, the inspiration and the joy of it.

All through life he had to endure the discipline of fettering ill-health ; even reading was often forbidden. Yet he tore through book after book, seemingly with one glance wresting the heart out of it. But seldom was anybody conscious of what he was enduring, so conspicuous was the triumph of spirit over substance.

Henry Scott Holland was born in 1847 ; his father hunted and travelled after the old English type of a " gentleman at large," his mother a daughter of Lord Gifford ; his boyhood's home was in Warwickshire, and later at Wimbledon. Nothing here to account for this man. Far away in the recesses of the past somewhere or somewhen there must have been exciting unusual ancestors—who can tell ? At Eton he was a normal, manly boy, full of fun and charm, but showing no special intellectual power. But the unique relations between the boy and his tutor, the well-known William Johnson, prove that he was of no ordinary mould. His tutor, as every one knows, was a peculiarly fine and delicate scholar, a poet and a historian, brilliant in many directions, with the eccentricity of a genius, whose power of discovering and drawing out a boy's character and intellect never has been surpassed. Lytteltons and Gladstones, the Woods, the Primroses, passed under his influence and sway and owed much to his stimulating power. Then, as ever since, Holland's moral standard was of the highest, and no evil thing, or impurity of thought, word or deed dared manifest itself in his presence. He attracted some of the most

notable Etonians of the period—chief among them
the brother of the present Lord Halifax, the enchanting Freddy Wood, and Dalmeny, afterwards Lord
Rosebery, " the beloved Archie," as his tutor calls
him.

" There was nothing to comfort me," wrote William Johnson, " in parting with Holland (on Holland's leaving Eton), " to him I could say nothing,
and now that I am writing about it, I cannot bear to
think that he is gone." [1]

But it was at Balliol that his brain began to be
discovered. To Jowett he owed nothing ; but the
wise and profound T. H. Green quickly recognised
the powers and possibilities of his mind, and came
to delight in his brilliant pupil. Green was the first
to discover the philosopher that smouldered within
the youth. Holland quickly caught fire, and would
in after life have pointed to Green as his guide and
master. " Yet never," as Dr. Gore pointed out,
" was his mind enslaved even by Green."

Athletics played no mean part in his career—he
rowed in his College eight, jumped unparalleled
heights, steered the Torpid, was incomparable as a
swimmer and a skater. But it was philosophy that
became his absorbing interest. All ideas of a diplo-
matic career were swept away in the flood of Plato
and Aristotle, Hegel and Green. He was described

---

[1] " Letters and Journals," by William Cory (at that time Johnson).

in those days as absorbed in Ruskin and Browning, deeply exercised by social problems and the miseries of the East End, always unconventional, forming friendships with all and sundry, devoted to music, and passionately interested in labour questions. " One could not bear it unless one knew there was another world," was the rather trite remark made to him by a lady as they came out into the crowd from a gay London party. " *Are we to have both then?* " he said.

His First in " Greats " was a surprise to many, and his *viva voce* was described as so brilliant a performance that one of the examiners declared that he had never heard anything to be compared to it. It was while still an undergraduate that his craving for a closer union with God resulted in a resolution to take Holy Orders. At Peterborough, under the mystic but sometimes mystifying Westcott, he studied theology during a long vacation. His work at Christ Church did not allow of his being a student at Cuddesden, but its College, presided over by the Saint, Dr. King (afterwards Bishop of Lincoln), had an irresistible attraction for all that was most romantic and spiritual in Holland's nature. It was in 1872 that he was ordained, and from that time the sermons he preached in Oxford were described by a freshman of the day as absolutely original and pertaining to himself alone, filled with light, movement and colour.

With great rapidity he became Student and Tutor of Christ Church, Select Preacher to the University, Senior Proctor, a new and brilliant star in the Oxford sky, a Captain and a Leader, breaking up a certain deadness that had depressed the University.

In December, 1873, Dr. Liddon, then Canon of St. Paul's, selected Holland, the young deacon, to preach in the great Cathedral, little dreaming of the long and glorious connection that was eventually to be his with the centre of the world's concourse.

When in 1884 Mr. Gladstone offered him the Canonry at St. Paul's, it was universally felt that the Prime Minister had matched a great opportunity with a great man. London welcomed him as a remarkable and stimulating preacher ; a literary critic of unique skill and power, a teacher in many regions outside theology, a counsellor in difficulty, a comforter in distress, inspiring in his friendships, and one of the most vivid and joyous figures in social life.

After twenty-seven years at St. Paul's he left London and returned to Oxford. Mr. Asquith, in 1910, made him Regius Professor of Divinity, and there for the last eight years he lived, to exercise a wonderful attraction for the young men who came in contact with him. His deepest conviction was that in religion only could be solved the practical problems of the world. And he faced them with a courage that never swerved, with a faith that never faltered. He had no use for those who shirked—he faced life as he found it surging all around him.

As the inspired interpreter of the Bible perhaps he stood alone : through all his thought and action could be seen his Christ-centred philosophy, because of the intimate contact of his passionate heart with life's contemporary drama. " Though we shall no longer see him leading the Christian armies to victory, or rallying them when discouraged or dismayed, he still marches forward, and still his hope and energy and prophetic fire are given to the service of his Master." [1]

There is a quality impossible to analyse or to communicate, and this it was that distinguished Dr. Holland from all others—he had genius.

This slight sketch of the progress of his days, however inadequate, may be useful as a background. The life that has been written of him,[2] the tributes and testimonies of his countless friends, will fill up the gaps. But, indeed, it matters little when and where he was born, whether he was with or without pedigree or posterity, in what places he dwelt, what work he had to do. Like all souls chosen of God, he was independent of time and place, of circumstance, or

---

[1] Dr. William Temple, Bishop of Manchester.
[2] " Memoir and Letters of Henry Scott Holland," published 1921, edited by Stephen Paget.

heredity or environment. He was a miracle, a meteor, one of those astonishing beings that happen once in a century, dropped from the clouds, to renew a perplexed and worn-out world, to startle it out of humdrum ways, and inspire it to take up life's song anew. I know that we should beware of anything that seems like exaggeration. But think as I must, search as I may, in this man I can discover no flaw. Some lack of balance, of proportion, may possibly at times have been the outcome of the enthusiastic nature of his temperament. But this hardly pertains to character. Human he was to the last degree, with a passion of pity that knew no limit. Stern as he was with sin, or even with compromise, with the sinner he was infinitely merciful.

One of the most delightful traits in his character was his power of friendship equally with old and young, with one generation after another—all were equally certain of his sympathy, help and advice. " In his company were himself and you only, and the whole wide world for playground and exploration." Ever as young as the youngest, he was ahead of them, ahead of his day. His was the genius to give and evoke life. He was a seer, he could divine. He was a prophet, he could foresee—his was a brain so wide in its sweep, so deep in its understanding. Perhaps I may here quote a letter written in 1917, just after his death, to one who loved him greatly, even though he was the greatest friend of her mother. He was her own greatest friend, and in course of becoming her children's greatest friend.

Of all the many people to be most lovingly remembered and pitied in losing our dearest H. S. H., you perhaps come first and foremost to my mind. For it was a friendship that lasted from your cradle to his grave. To you he gave the tender love of a grown man for a little child : as you grew into maidenhood, this developed into the perfect guardianship, the love of a brother and a father, stimulating, guiding, guarding all that was growing in you—and then the last stage, in some ways the most perfect, as you reached the crown of womanhood in love and marriage and motherhood. And still you could count on that miraculous vitality, fun and freshness—an affection uniting the enthusiasm of the boy, the youth and the man, ripened by age, judgment and experience, and still the greatest friend of yourself, your mother, and your children. There has been all along for you this unequalled devotion, spirit and faith to lean on, always ready for you. How can we ever render thanks enough for this great gift that has been ours for so many years ?

Remember, O Lord Jesus, ever and always, with Thy most merciful love and compassion, him who was so dear to us, and for whose memory we give Thee humble and hearty thanks.

Of his preaching some people might hastily assume that the rush, the torrent of his words were, as in the case of a popular preacher of his time, used to veil the poverty of his thought. Dr. Gore thinks that some of our intellectuals allowed themselves to be deluded by the rhetorical look of his sermons into not taking him seriously as a thinker. There could be no greater mistake. For there was in him what Dr. Gore calls " a profound philosophical and theological mind, a fine intuition, which interpreted with wonderful sureness the inner heart of the facts. Never was he satisfied with *a priori* reasoning. His intellectual joy lay in examining the fact till the idea behind revealed itself to him. His mind was pre-eminently original ; there never was in him anything secondhand or second-rate—no borrowed goods at all."

He was a man of ideas, he had too many ideas. Often they swept him off the main path into side tracks. To his hearers he was frequently difficult to follow, there was no time. He tore along and they were carried breathlessly after him. He suggested more than he developed or explained, he gave his listeners hard work to keep up with him. His power of expression was surely unique—the whirl, the wealth of ideas, of analogy, of illustration, of antithesis, of simile.

That cataract of words would consist of argument, appeal, consecutive reasoning on a high plane, interpenetrated with humour, with poetic imagery, with an extraordinary felicity of phrase, which made not only for the kindling of emotion and the exercise of personality, but also for the sense of commanding intellect, sure of itself and of the world. It

was as a prophet that he preached, testifying in the heart of
the capital of the Empire, amidst its splendours and its
squalors, against its amazing materialism.[1]

The unforgettable tones of his voice ! And then,
suddenly, with one sweeping gesture of extraordinary
nobility, a gesture which seemed to enfold and
embrace the whole of suffering humanity, he would
break into a brief, burning prayer.

It was only the year before his death that he
poured out his soul in a series of inspiring sermons at
St. Paul's, Knightsbridge. Well do I remember—
as I heard him preach—how accurately the description written to me thirty years earlier still exactly
applied. In was in January, 1888, when Dr. Holland was in the full meridian of his power, that Alfred
Lyttelton heard him preach in St. Paul's Cathedral.
Word for word the description held good in 1917,
when Dr. Holland was seventy.[1]

I have just come [Alfred wrote] from St. Paul's, and my
brains are still dancing and my heart burning with Holland's
sermon. I think, on the whole, it is the finest I ever heard.
He never left the ancient ways, but yet illumined them with
floods of new light. He was generally restrained in language,
but when he broke loose, we blessed the weakness of his
fetters. He was rarely rhetorical, but there was a sustained
eloquence throughout—an epigrammatic felicity and a clean-
ness, vigour, and completeness about the argument, often
like a great enthusiastic judge. It is impossible to summarise,

[1] Rt. Hon. C. F. G. Masterman.

because the ideas were so abundant, that we never had time to put the last into any of memory's strong cells. It is useless to try and give you the barest outline—and possibly publication might spoil it, so intense was the spirit of him, diffused by his yearning voice and passionate gestures. Yet I trust I may never forget it.

Time has quickly passed since the death of Alfred Lyttelton. The war seems to have obliterated all sense of time and space. Some words of Dr. Holland's on Alfred Lyttelton may be fitly recalled, describing an evening in Exeter College, Oxford, early in the year 1885:

When he stood up in his beautiful manhood to speak to undergraduates on behalf of the White Cross League— could anything have been more manly, more gracious, more winning ? He could speak on such a topic with the perfect certainty and confidence of a man who knew how to come through the fire.

PART II

Here, perhaps, may be quoted a few passages from Dr. Holland's letters or writings, words of wit or wisdom that linger in the memory.

Tintern Abbey.   1869.

You may talk about Milan till you are black in the face ; but you will never know what a Church can be till you have been to that Abbey on the Wye.   It is ridiculous to call it a ruin : and even if it has no roof, or pavement, or oak stalls, or choristers, the blue sky covers it, and the green grass enamels it, the hanging ivy drapes it, and the birds carol and chant in it. . . . The whole stands among the hills like a visible hymn, a prayer that has taken bodily shape.

Ruskin.   1870.

He has raised audiences that would have made Mat. Arnold's head a foot higher : the whole theatre crammed : it really is the most gorgeous eloquence it is possible to hear ; it makes one perspire, it is so beautiful.

Jenny Lind.   1870.

Jenny Lind was a wonder and a joy.   She passed *through* life.   That is what she made one feel : she was on her way somewhere else : it was a movement across a scene—her life.   On she passed : often in perplexity and surprise at what she found here.   Never quite at home : never comfortable, and settled, and at rest.   On she went travelling :

and as she passed she left all eyes following after her, and all hearts wondering after her, as after a sudden vision.

Sunrise in Switzerland. 1871.

We strode on silently and solemnly, as the moon gradually paled and the dawn grew greeny-grey and brindled, and the lines of the crags began to get sharp and jagged against the eastern sky : on and on we went, as if the sun never would rise, till at last the little flying wisps of cloud blushed and crimsoned, and then a tinge stole over the head of the Matterhorn and the Mischabel, and then peak after peak caught it and passed it on, and the grand snowfields were diffused with warmth and colour. . . . And up he came, the great High King of Nature, like a bridegroom out of his chamber, rejoicing like a giant to run his course.

To a Boy Chosen to " Cox " One of the Eton Eights. 1872.

Now you have taken your place in the little (or great ?) world of Eton, you are a real *bonâ fide* " personage " with a definite dignity in the school hierarchy. What a noble swell ! a live steerer. Good gracious, why there is little more in life worth having after that !

Such a jolly life, too, with the eight swinging along bounding after you, and you feel it lift out of the water, and the stream curdles with that most delicious of all noises under the bending oars, and oh ! how the bank flies by you as you tear along in the stream that catches you coming out of old Boren Lock, sneaking along close to the shore which dances with all its daisies and dandelions as you whirl away to the Hopes. Then, too, the long sweet hours on Monkey Island, twining the dog-roses in your hat ; and the 4th of June with all the glory of white-ducks and gigantic bouquets, and the wild spin in the dark down the black-gliding waters through the misty shadowy banks, whirling along till you come with a rush into the roar and blare and yelling crowd and phizzing fire-works and pealing bells and flashing lights of the Brocas. Ah, how lovely it all is. . . .

Boy Friendships. 1872.

Believe me, friendship between big and little boys can be as good and pure as any ; it is capable of endless good to both, and there is a charm in it sometimes which is almost divine. The little boy may do more good than he imagines if he keeps his head steady and his heart pure. The bigger boy will reverence him and like to learn of him.

Rejoice in your youth and in the pleasures of it ; only remembering that for all these things " God will bring you unto judgement."

Sorrow. 1872.

Sorrow has impressed me enormously lately : it does lift me into unknown worlds. But there it stops : I make nothing of it. It leaves me dumb with awe, but will not take any shape, or strike a definite truth into my soul—it will not do more than shadow out its message, then sweep by its dim vestures, without turning upon me the clear eyes of God. It will not mould itself into the Christian Faith and stamp its truth home to me.

His Ordination. 1872.

To my joy I was to read the Gospel, a great pleasure to rise and shout those magnificent words " Let your loins be girded about "—they seemed to express the whole meaning and glory of the service. I have seldom been happier than at the time of Ordination. All hankerings, all questionings vanished. . . . I know that I am bound to gird up every thought, wish, prayer, hope, tendency, inclination, love into the expectancy of the Lord I have sworn to serve.

Inviting a Preacher to St. Paul's Cathedral.

Would you like to preach in St. Paul's one evening in May at 7 o'clock to a guileless mass of clerks and sweethearts holding each others' hands and glad to use common hymn-books ? The people of St. Paul's are not purse-proud City gents who sit on rich farms dealing largely in horseflesh ; they are all humble folk who would take the message from you.

The Maconochie Judgement. 1878.

How delicious about the Privy Council and Maconochie. It is a most serious blow to that benighted body ; and to think that *The Times* even has recognised that Lay Lords totally ignorant of Ecclesiastical Law should not be the most perfect administrators of that Law ! It is wonderful ! and Lord Penzance—one wonders whether he will ever succeed in finding out what he is, where he may sit, or what judgement he may give.

On the Appointment of Dr. King to the Lincoln Bishopric. 1883.

The surprise and delight of King ! A St. Francis de Sales at Lincoln—a Joy like an old Spring, if you can fancy Spring grown old—a mellow Spring—a mature Spring—a gray-haired Spring—a wrinkled Spring—like a delicious old lady delicately dancing—an Anna-Miriam or a Miriam-Anna for four-score years on the steps of the Temple, in the Altar silences, yet with a flash and jingle of the timbrel about her head.

It is lovely as a dream—King moving through the dim fens, on a slow pacing cob—Blessing kneeling peasants—He will move as a benediction.

Gt. Chesterford Rectory.

Once more, after several little arrow flights of friends, Moberley for four days, an Indian for five, Paget for two, Stanton of Cambridge for one, here I am alone again till Friday, and am happy as a grig. It is delightful, so restful, so luxurious ; I suppose now that people marry wives, when they live alone, for fear of being too happy—for the sake of discipline—lest they should have no unpleasant duties. Otherwise, with a dog and a piano, the bliss would be too overpowering.

Bel Alp. 1883.

I have not yet sent you a line, but the Blue Gentians to-day were so speechlessly lovely that I had to pick two and send them to you, just to assure you that their colour is as surprising and overwhelming as ever. But alas ! they die ! . . . Dear old B. [his companion] is a splendid physical Clog : and there are no big mountaineers at all, but excellent people who go to daily Matins at 8 a.m. and who discover strange flowers ; and take out lunch with them ; and do the Pension 10/ frcs. Old Tyndal presides daily, and we all chatter and make great friends ; and, of course, everybody finds that he knows everybody else's grandmother. The weather is simply ridiculous. It is so fine that you almost throw a book at its head. Every Peak is as clear as a whistle from the time the sun rises until the full moon comes rolling up over Monte Leone, for you can see *inside* the Weisshorn and the Don.

In 1883 he was Invited to Accompany Mr. and Mrs. Gladstone, etc., in the " Pembroke Castle " Trip round Scotland to Norway and Denmark.

. . . Oh ! and the voyage ! How can I ? I am pledged. . . . And the ship ! I know those ships ! The huger they are the more awful the long, uplifting heave, and the more hideous the slow sinking subsidence in the unending abyss. How could I hang on the lips of the P.M. while my whole physical self was itself hung in dreadful suspense, on the top of each hanging wave ? So I must thank you heartily. It would have been " immense fun," as you say ; if only it had been on dry land ! Why do these ships go to sea ? They are most fascinating things in themselves : so bright and clean and gay. They spoil it all by going on the water. So it is always in life—the best things have some queer twist in them and get perverted.

St. Paul's Cathedral, February, 1884, just after His Appointment to a Canonry.

. . . That beautiful St. Paul's ! I went up to a great rushing roaring service on Monday night, splendid with music and light.

Wonderful to feel the first touch of " home " about it— to think one would be no interloper—or spectator—or accident—or casual performer hired by the night, but a real

" belonging," as good and real as a verger. The old Dome looked to me quite motherly : and I should like to have got up and kissed it.

Most noble and lovely home ! I shall love to go in and out and listen and watch !

Mr. Chamberlain's Face.   1884.

The compact outline had no suggestiveness, there seemed to be no inviting problems to be worked out : no attractive obscurities : no ins and outs : no minglings : no fancies : no dreams—you left off at the face—you never got deeper, the clean surface repelled enquiry—it simply asked you to take it or leave it just as you liked : after my best endeavours to be interested, I left off exactly where I began.

Invited to Meet Miss Laura Tennant just before Her Marriage in 1885.

I dare not—I am on the edge of a smash, and great as would be the delight of meeting Miss Laura again, she has never had the effect upon me of a wet bandage, of soothing and placid stupidity—this is what I really need,—something wide, stout, massive and asleep. She is not this, so far as I can recollect her.

Mr. Shorthouse's " John Inglesant,"   1885.

Ten years he brooded : and bit by bit he wrote and over it he hung : and round about it his imagination played : and his reason pondered : and he watered it with his anxieties : and he fed it with his hopes :. and he nursed it in his dreams and he fused it with the fires of his spiritual ardour. So there at last it emerged, with all this intensity of personal existence to quicken and ensoul it.

Travelling in 1886 with Mrs. Meynell Ingram in
Her Yacht, he wrote from Smyrna :

Every imaginable face and leg turn up in the bazaars here,
and through them all sad camels squeeze their lumbering
dismal way ; they look overwhelmed with the pathos of
their position, their skins don't fit, their joints come anywhere
and anyhow : their hair seems to have been used up by John
the Baptist, who has only left them the locks and tufts that
were too bad even for him ; they despair of knowing how
their necks will stick on another minute, they feel sure they
are being led on some hopelessly futile errand, they are
almost determined to lie down and die at every step, but
they always put it off for one step more.

Dr. Temple. 1886.

I rejoice that you love that strong lion of a Bishop, with
his hoarse roar, and his jungle of whiskers, and his rock-like
face : yet so noble, and tender, and true, and powerful : he
always makes me cry with joy that earth holds any one so
spiritually great.

Written anonymously for Walter de la Mare, then a
Chorister at St. Paul's Cathedral, and published
in the " Choristers' Journal " late in 1889.

LYRICAL RHAPSODY.

Here they are the children
Of the big blue dome,
All agog to utter
Thoughts that go and come.

Gray old frowsy fogies
   Try to make a noise
By writing in the paper,
   Why not then the boys ?

Why should only old blokes
   Wield the pen and ink ;
Why should not the young folks
   Tell us what they think ?

Must your head be hairless
   Ere you're fit to spout ;
Must your mouth be shut until
   Your teeth are out ?

No ! let Deans and Canons
   Write their fusty books,
Cawing there, and croaking
   Like a pack of rooks.

Our young brains are teeming
   With words as good as theirs,
Our young heads are steaming
   With thoughts too deep for tears.

Out then with our stilo !
   Give us each a pen,
We can do the business
   Quite as well as men.

Let those ancient fogies
   See what we can do
While our chins are hairless,
   While our souls are new.

While we're in a glutter
　　How on earth to spell
All we want to utter,
　　All we've got to tell.

Hurrah ! for the Cathedral
　　And three cheers for the Dean,
For here's the second number
　　Of the Boy's Own Magazine.

In the summer of 1887 we were sharing in an almost historic reading party in the Jura Mountains : Dr. Talbot, Dr. Gore, Dr. Holland, Arthur Lyttelton, Herbert Trench, and some Oxford undergraduates —threading her winsome way through this company was a curly-headed child of five : [1]

Wonderful, wondering, winsome Winny,
Who whether at luncheon, or breakfast, or dinny
Scatters the jam all over her pinny,
　　Till no one can say
　　At the end of the day
Which is the jam pot and which is Winny.

Chorus of gentlemen.
And which is the sweetest, the jam or Winny !

" And which is the sweetest ? " asked Winny, after listening to the poem. " The jams, of course," was the reply.

The following letter is also addressed to her.　On

---

[1] Youngest daughter of Dr. Talbot, Bishop of Winchester.

A.　　　　　　　　　　　　　　　　　　　　　　　G

the way from Hawarden, where he had parted from
Winny, he wrote, October, 1887 :—

I passed Oxford yesterday, and all the towers and spires
came rushing down to the station, with all their bells jostling
and crying, "How's Winny?" "Here is a man who
has seen Winny! Oh Winny, Winny!" And old Tom
came puffing along and growled out, very deep, "How's
Winny?" and the little Keble dinner-bell ran up and
whispered in my ear, "Does she get enough jam?" and
then they all went on singing nothing but "Winny, Winny,
Winny."

. . . I can't think how I should have got away from them,
as they all clung about my neck, crying "Winny, Winny,
Winny," and poor old St. Mary's spire quite broke down,
and Magdalen tower sobbed aloud—but the train rushed on
and tore me away, poor St. Philip's holding on to me to the
last minute : and still the little voices kept following me,
saying "Winny, Winny." You must go round to each of
them when you get back, and give them a kiss ; they will be
so pleased. Good-bye, little gossamer thing.

February, 1888. Dr. Warre had promised to preach at St. Paul's Cathedral.

I will gladly act host to you on behalf of St. Paul . . . the
congregation like the preacher to go slow. They form a
compact mass of *excellent Philistines*, solid ranks of tradesmen
and wives, the people who "ride in buses," and they listen
readily to the plain Gospel.

Written from Hawarden, where he had gone to speak to Young Men. 1891.

We had a very successful meeting in the new Gymnasium,
and it was a great joy to speak to the men. Then we had a

superb exhibition, eight Liverpool heroes over, performing magnificent and most thrilling feats. The G.O.M. came, charged with earnest attention. He was wonderfully noble, and dignified, and simple : old, but full of splendid force, with his eye flashing and thunders in his voice. He is absorbed in his new library.

In 1895 he wrote of the First Death in the Cathedral Choir School :

We buried him with lovely wailing music from all his little mates. He was a *bewildering flutter* of gaiety and innocence.

On receiving a Hawarden Photograph of the Family on Bicycles. 1896.

Dossie on wheels is delightful. Like a Summer insect, fluttery, and wispish, and quaint and winning—just the thing a Salmon would rise at, hovering over a sunny pool— I am that Salmon, in a long black coat, rising at the Fairy Fly.

The West Window in Hawarden Church, by Burne Jones, to be placed by the sons and daughters of Mr. and Mrs. Gladstone as a thanksgiving for the long lives of their parents. It was only completed and placed in the church one week after Mr. Gladstone's death and one week before the death of Sir E. Burne Jones.

And as to the West Window at Hawarden and its subject, the great Benedicite—O William, O Catherine, with all your children and grandchildren, and Dossies and Flossies, bless ye the Lord : praise Him, and magnify Him for ever.

After the funeral in Westminster Abbey, May 28, 1898, some members 'of Mr. Gladstone's family had expressed regret for the unprotected position of the grave in the open gangway in the North Transept. H. S. Holland wrote :

I would far, far rather have it out in the open under the passing feet than hidden away beneath the benches. Is it not part of the honour of lying there, in the Abbey, that all London and England, and all the world tread above your grave ? He lies there in the thick of the throng. Ever the feet pass over him—the tramp of the multitudes. All the great ones who lie there are become the property of the people. . . . Of course the sweet peace and reserve of a quiet corner in dear Hawarden Churchyard is lost. But you would not wish his body to be elsewhere than in the great Church of the Nation.[1]

In 1903 Dr. Holland went on a Mission to South Africa. He wrote :

In the midst of the Sea.

The sea grey, but never rising out of a manageable flatness. It is miraculous. We dance, we play, we go to church, we do nothing at all for hours with qualified success. . . . How long this amazing calm will last, I cannot tell. The sea is the most strangely foolish thing I have ever met : such a lot of it, with nothing on earth to do. What is it there for ?

The Unemployed at St. Paul's. 1905.

Of course, if the men will come on a Sunday, they are bound to find themselves in face of the normal Cathedral

[1] " Letters from Henry Scott Holland."

service, which is very elaborate and remote. . . . Anyhow, the sweet music rose and fell, and the lights shone and the lessons from Isaiah and Revelation shot out, and the hymns rolled, and the organ thundered ; and the men sat, and looked, and thought, and were warm, and rested tired limbs, and felt not wholly un-at-home in God's house.

After the death of his Sister. 1906.

All else is dark. But the Sacrament this morning had somehow its old strength of assurance : it seemed to make all things clean, body and spirit alike. And it bade us at all times, however blind, at all places in our lives, however clouded, to give thanks, and to sing out " Holy, Holy, Holy . . ."

It means the passing out of the inner secret of our home joy. She was its spring. Always dear, cheerful, fresh, sweet, tender, quick. Every thought of her is blessed : every memory good. Fifty perfect years. Thank God.

Good-bye to his home at Wimbledon. 1908.

I was away, saying good-bye to Gayton Lodge. It goes on May 1st. It will be my last sight of the poor old place. Forty-seven years of life flung away behind ! It is a big uprooting. All the memories of father, mother, brother, sister—all dead. I went round the rooms : and prayed. So ugly the Victorian house. Yet charged with tenderness. And I have loved the Common—with its windy breadths of brown colour. The poor brother is very sad ; packing, ning, clearing. So I could not have seen you. God bless

1.

To Gwladys—His Lost Surplice.   1908.

Had you not better confess at once ?   That surplice of
mine.   It was too tempting.   It would make up so beautifully
as a dear little white frock for a ball.   Just a bit cut down
at the neck.   Just a tucker taken in at the waist.   Just a
pucker in the flounce.   One red rose in front ;   and a fringe
let in round the skirt.

Chopin.   1908.

Nobody has the soul of a piano in him like Chopin.   He
feels, and thinks, and talks, just as a piano would if it were
alive.   And then the playing of him must be so delicious.
He is plaintive, is he not ?   Something tender, and half
crying, and pitiful, as if his heart strings were very delicate
and high strung.   It is the sort of sadness which you hear
in some birds' notes, and in winds blowing round crannied
corners, when they pipe like lost children.

Gwladys.   1908.

My Gladys—no, Gwladys—that is much jollier.   It is
like a gurgle of water out of a bottle with a narrow neck.   It
is like the dying sound of a lamp going out.   It is like a gurgle
that has failed to come off and has ended in a splutter.   It
is full of all happy noises as of birds gloating with joy over
early worms ;   and of bubbles that burst ;   and of odd watery
gulps where a rat has dived. . . .

A Bust of Cardinal Newman.   1908.

It has got the old touch in the face and the beautiful
forehead.   You remember the sculptor who said that everybody else's head after Newman's felt like a turnip ?   It is
very gentle, and the face has a look of the old labourer at

the cottage door, which Arthur Lyttelton noticed in Cardinal
Newman long ago, the sad quiet wistfulness, and a little
bewildered at a world which had been so odd to him.

After reading Compton Mackenzie's " Carnival." 1912.

Jenny is the one and only thing in the book : a wonderful
attempt to give the Atalanta virginity in this whiff of a girl.

A Message to a Mutual Friend. 1912.

Do beg her to measure the depth of my regard by the
length of my silence.

On a Friend with a Bony Face. 1913.

Frank was so thin that one could have shaved oneself
with his head and face.

Graves. 1915.

Graves are empty things : they do nothing for one, except
just serve to symbolize tenderness and affection. . . .
Anyhow, do not trouble over your " gravelessness." But
there must be an effort to make it intelligible to the poor
maids, remembering that their whole minds and hearts go
out to the graves. If you can do anything to set them at ease
about them by some sort of kindly attention to the poor spot,
it would be happier for them.

To a Friend on her Seventieth Birthday. 1917.

I saw her fifty years ago,
A rosebud just about to blow—
And now she comes our hearts to fill,
A Granny—but a rosebud still.

At a Meeting while he was a Canon.

What can we do with our old Canons ? You can make harness out of old horses, and you can make Bovril out of old cows. But is there anything you can make out of old Canons ?

(This naturally led to a visit of indignation from the Bovril representatives.)

Once upon a time (November, 1884), after listening to " Parsifal " at the Albert Hall, Mr. Mackail walked home with me to Downing Street (he being at that time incongruously caged in a Government Office). We were speaking of H. S. Holland in terms of much appreciation.

" The only drawback I find in him," said my friend, " is the extreme difficulty of knowing whether he is serious or in fun. A few days ago I was at a meeting of the Oxford Browning Society. ' The Flight of the Duchess ' was the subject. Arthur Sidgwick read the opening paper interpreting the Gipsy as a Lover. Holland had already written his ' Note,' but his indignation being aroused by (as he thought) so despicable a solution, he—while Sidgwick was speaking—hurriedly scribbled down a different conclusion to his own already-written paper. It was brilliantly witty and amusing, but how much of it did he mean ? "

On the next day I wrote to H. S. H. and begged

for a look at the " Note." He sent it to me by return
of post, with apologies for so unreadable a pencil
scrawl, so great a caricature was it even of his own
handwriting.

To Mr. Mackail the world owes the preservation
from death and burial of this enchanting effusion,
which is printed, for the first time, at the end of this
chapter.

Part III

It was said by a distinguished divine, in attempting
to differentiate between Dr. Holland's gifts, that as a
conversationalist he undoubtedly came first, next on
the platform, last in the pulpit. There is truth in a
remark I heard last spring—" The mistake people
made about Holland was in trying to get him to
preach. They ought to have tried to get him to
dine." In discussion he revelled, and nobody could
be more exhilarating, even intoxicating. But into
argument you could not inveigle him—he regarded
argument between those who held opposite opinions
as waste of time, waste of powder—it left the com-
batants where they started, it did not accord with
his sense of perspective, or indeed with his sense of
humour. There was in him the imperishable child.
He never really quite grew up.

There was little of the recluse about him—he
made himself felt wherever he was as a vivid and
active force. He was a fount of joy to all who came
across him. Yet he never sought happiness—in
giving it to others he received it himself. In spite of
his brilliant talk, in spite of his fun, behind the
laughter and the flashing repartee, his real home lay
in another world. He was a mystic : at home in the

many mansions of his Father's house : at home in
the regions of the unseen : ever in touch with the
eternal verities. His soul had learnt by resolute
practice the habit of retreating into the spiritual
recesses that lie behind our mortal life. In speaking
of a friend who had passed beyond the veil, he used
words which to us seem almost a picture of his own
experience. In the mystical life he describes the
strong " need of self discipline and correction, the
need of balance, of control, of loyalty to the forms of
institutional religion, the steadying compensation of
Church order, of loyalty to her Sacraments." Never
did he fail the demands made upon him, but it was
in the secret recesses, in the silences of his soul, that
he was able to find the peace that passeth understanding.

How rare it was for him to speak of himself !
Only on one occasion can I recall it. In 1883 he
wrote :—

If one could know beforehand what would be said after
death of one, how quickened and uprising life would become.
To learn what others looked for in you—what they found —
what they missed—this would be an immense and inspiring
gain.

Of this he must have had a foretaste on his very
death-bed. A short note has been published, written
on February 6th, 1917, in quick and grateful
response to a letter sent to him by one who owed

much to him. " I lay your words to my heart and treasure them there. I am low and beaten, and I cannot tell you what healing comfort you bring to my soul—though indeed I cannot believe half you say."

Can there be a more fitting conclusion than a free rendering of some passages from the tribute paid to him by his friend and disciple, Philip Waggett,[1] at St. Matthew's, Westminster ? I choose those words that came home to me most, that found an echo in my own heart, that must have found an echo in the hearts of those who listened. Rather than quote them word for word I have absorbed them, identified them with my own thoughts of him, and in a sense ventured to make them my own :

My life has been led from week to week, from year to year, by stages of the hope of finding Holland again, in Christ Church, or at Amen Court, or in Hoxton, or Cambridge, or wherever the cause of the poor was to be urged and the claim of the Kingdom of God to be declared—one of the band of his children to whom, so far, the deepest interest and the greatest thrill of life has been to speak to Holland. Close as he seemed to us, as life went on a space appeared between him and us, a space untraversed even by his abounding sympathy and the strong

[1] Father Philip Waggett, S.S.J.E.

flight of his eloquence. His Divine philosophy must stand as the great achievement of his life. Loss must for a time result from the swiftness and urgency of his mental movement, from a certain solitude in his adventure of thought and faith. Thirty years ago he offered us answers to problems which were not, at that time, recognised or urgent. He was always ahead of his time, yet he lost no key to the present or the past. And now that the problems are in the very air we breathe, and are realised with something like fear and dread, men are groping for even a part of what he long ago set before us. He has been taken away from the evil day. We shall need him when the time of achievement comes, when the conscience of a great nation in victory must ring true to what is now the prayer of a great nation in adversity ; we shall need his sternness, his integrity, his prophetic instinct, his grasp of facts, his exacting judgment, his wonderful voice. How we shall miss him when the day comes of our deliverance and of our triumph, a day fraught with the peril of forgetfulness—Lest we forget :

> The tumult and the shouting dies—
>   The Captains and the Kings depart—
> Still stands Thine ancient sacrifice,
>   An humble and a contrite heart.
> Lord God of Hosts be with us yet,
>   Lest we forget—lest we forget.

" This is the disciple which testifieth of these things, and we know that his testimony is true." This man also—in Christ, under St. John, in that great army led by the Apostles—this man also, in his time, for his task, in his place and in his scale, is a disciple who bore witness for Christ : who saw the Water and the Blood, who knew the pardon and the life, who felt the passion of God and the power of the Spirit. With the voice of a man, with the love of a friend, and with the illuminating, persuading force of a present teacher, he taught of God, testified of the glory of Christ, and we know that his testimony is true.

We know that it is genuine. We know that it is not only genuine in temper, but true in substance, we who have knelt with him in the Sacrament of Penitence, we who have risen from his blessing refreshed, renewed, we who found perplexities and problems disentangled by his counsel, we whose minds he led in every crisis, he led to Christ and Christ alone—we, too, have won a share of light and of conviction.

Every one knows his charm, the perpetual delight of his wit, his abounding light and grace and fun, his astonishing sympathy and insight, his generosity, his passion for the poor—even strangers must have felt his welcoming heart, must have been penetrated by this brightness, this quickening thought, this amazing stimulation of the mind, this better than stimulant, this tonic for heart and brain which was Holland. There was no other. We can never see his like. Yet the sound of his greatness has been drowned in the song of his charm. His greatness is not fully acknowledged or recognised. He was the greatest man, when he died, then standing in England. His greatness found a joy in reflecting the greatness of Gladstone. These two stand out on the scale and pattern of heroes, carrying heavier metal of personality, greater guns, more power to inspire and to strike.

I confess to a sense of impatience when I hear Holland compared with this Bishop or that Dean, with this writer or that preacher. He did not belong to the same mould. He was of a different scale, of a more august chapter of design. This was our witness, this was our friend, who saw further than we could, who told us the truth. It was because he was wrapped in the sense of the awful Majesty of God that his soul flew out to meet the souls of other saints of his stature, men of the unseen, pilgrims of eternity, Patriot Citizens of the Kingdom of GOD.

Being thus great and strong, he bore witness of the pardoning love of Christ, of the inexhaustible treasure of the Divine compassion, of the all-prevailing virtue of the Precious Blood. There is no sin but Christ's Passion can touch it, there is no treason but Christ's faithfulness can redeem it, there is no degradation but Christ's risen life can transform it. Such was Holland, a full channel from the Eternal Fount of courage and of joy. May he forgive us for speaking of him, of him whom we have never heard speak once of himself. May he forgive us.

" The long strain of his life here, a strain always intense and agonising, closed in great peace. He rests.—"

APPENDIX

The Flight of the Duchess.

It is the old familiar story—why should it need a note ? Surely it is not we in Oxford, who need to be instructed in the nature of that sharp contrast which we know only too nearly—the contrast between the stiff and ordered mechanism of an ancient Society, so arid with conventionalism—so yellow with thin and acrid discomfort—heavy as frost, burdensome with its weary routine of worn-out imitation—this—and then on the other side, the touch of divine madness—the ecstasy of the prophet—the heat of young and primæval inspirations, the sweet, large human air of Bohemian freedom—the unwithering Hope of the New World, that still draws Ulysses, weary and grey though he be, out of safe havens over wide and plunging seas—the magic of Wandering—the Passion for Liberty—the mysterious secret of the homeless Gipsy.

The crossing of these two lives is one of Browning's main motives—this wonder of momentary inspiration inside the habitual commonplace. He has its triumph in " By the Fireside " :

> " O the little more . . .
> And the little less, and what worlds away."

The Secret flashes : the Earth and Sky bend in one—the supreme Passion leaps out in one throb—now it is upon you ! That is the Hour to seize ! Lay hold ! and the life has been lifted to the new level : it has purpose and unity—truth from that moment unto Eternity. He writes out its failure—its fatal refusal in the " Byron de nos jours "—the two who wander together by the little grey Chapel over the Sea, where the gulls flap—and they are touched for the moment by the Invisible, and the Secret is disclosed—and the Veil lifts—and the Face looks through—and the thrill of Fate brushes over them—and they—they stop and reflect—they consider, they cannot offer themselves to the Motion of the Hour : they hold back : they lapse—and lo ! it is gone ! and the chance is withdrawn, and they are lost.

It is said, in its most violently paradoxical form, in the " Statue and the Bust "—the reverse of our present poem— the story of the two who fail to act under the inspiration of the Crisis, and therefore *fail*, indeed fail by the measure of the Saints—those Saints who burn on " row on row "—fail by *that* measure, even though the act they fail to do is *the worst of sins*.

And now, to-night, we have the perfect Victory of Inspiration, the Victory of the Gipsy Queen over all causes and rules, over all bonds and obligations, over all customs and proprieties, as well ecclesiastical as civil, in these her dominions supreme—the justification, without any after-thoughts allowed us, of the Bohemianism that there is in all the

A· H

Prophets ; and of the Prophesy that there is in all Bohemianism.

It is justified by the same Canon as that by which Wordsworth, the sober Priest of Duty, justified Burns' treatment of Tam o' Shanter's drunkenness. The poet, trusting to primary instincts, luxuriates among the felicities of love and wine. " I pity him who cannot perceive that in all this, though there is no moral purpose, there is moral effect :

> " Kings may be blest, but Tam was glorious—
> O'er all the ills of life victorious."

And—if you had to state the Difference ? . . .

Wherein lies the most vital *contrast* between the world of dead Convention—and the world of Living Inspiration ? In the contrast between the piece-meal and fragmentary disorder of the one and the sequent and unbroken and orderly Unity of the other. The lines in which Browning embodies his motive seem to me those in which he tells of the unity given to detached words, first by the under-breathing inspiration of music—and then, as this dropped, by the yet fuller under-Breath of the Gipsy's magical Sway :

> " The self-same contagion gained me
> And I kept time to the wondrous chime,
> Making out words and prose and rhyme,
> Till it seemed that the music furled
> Its wings like a task fulfilled, and dropped
> From under the words it first had propped.
> And left them mid-way in the world,
> Word took word, as hand takes hand
> I could hear at last and understand,
> And when I held the unbroken thread
> The Gipsy said . . ."

Here is the symbol. Words stand off by themselves, midway in the world, stiff and stark and alone—detached from one another by gaps and gulfs—hard—unyielding—stupid—in bits, until the music enters—the incantation—the contagion—with wings and breath, to *prop* the outward words, until " word takes word, as hand takes hand " and the whole is made one ; and they who can yield themselves to the Contagion find that they learn and understand and hold at last " the unbroken thread." The world of *habit* is all a mass of broken pieces—hard, stiff, detached—unadapting—unyielding—untouching—into which mob of wearisome and purposeless repetition souls are thrust, like the soul of that sweet " little lady "—for when there is nothing at all to be done in that Castle, where each post had already a man, and she was only to be part of the regulated mechanism—now by rule outside the hall, now in it—" to sit thus, stand thus, see and be seen," " at the proper place, in the proper minute," " and die away the life between " . . . So we find ourselves ; and we, too, do as she did—the little lady—who grew silent and thin :

> " Paling and ever paling
> As the way is with a hid chagrin."

And the world, like the Duke, perceives that we are dull and ailing, and says in its heart :

> " It's all done to spite me,
> But I shall find in my power to right me . . ."

All is loose and in pieces—until the blessed Contagion strikes in : and some breath, like music, sweeps through to prop and carry, and all the stiff bits of broken customs begin to grow together—and habit takes habit, as hand takes hand—and all is in touch—one with another—and we who have passed under the sway and swing of the great Incantation, we hear, and know, and understand—

" And hold at last the unbroken thread."

Where are our Duchesses—our " little ladies " ?   I should not so much go to search for them where our Poet friend has, in high-soaring castles, among tufted trees, behind the portcullis and the bastion.   No, I should turn to more familiar haunts.   I should knock at door after door, down long drear rows of semi-detached villas, by Norwood and Clapham Rise—by Putney and Turnham Green.   That is where they sit, thousands of little Duchesses—boxed in little square rabbit hutches.   Each has come there, a young bride, like this little bride—

" Active, stirring, all fire,
    Could not rest, could not tire,"

and has found like her that

" She who could do it great or small,
    She was to do nothing at all."

Nothing in the world to be done—all the places are long ago filled up.   She is only there to " meet her husband's eye " when he comes back fatigued, and bored with business.

" To sit thus, stand thus, and be seen
    At the proper place in the proper minute."

Nothing at all to do—nothing but the heartless trifling of a ridiculous social Routine—the Routine prescribed by all the other little Duchesses " Shut up in their own little rabbit

hutchesses " (a Rhyme that our Poet has somehow missed).
And

> " So these little ladies (on Clapham Rise) grow silent
>   and thin,
>   Paling and ever paling
> As the way is with a hidden chagrin."

The most striking parallel I have read lately to the tale of
our Duchess is a story by Julian Sturgis called " My Poor
Wife." [1] A wonderful picture of how it all happens, revealed
with entire unconsciousness by the husband's autobiography.
There no Gipsy steps in to the rescue—no Incantation
bewitches—and the " paling and ever paling " of the little
lady ends only in the last Wandering out into the unknown
land—ends only in the Mystery of the Enchantress *Death*.
It is a tale so natural, so pregnant, so near, so searching,
that those of us who look, from our high and secure Watch-
towers of Bachelorship, on those who toss in the wild and
stormy waters of Matrimony, would beg any wife to see that
any husband reads it.

And, since the first Note detected an allegory in our poem,
I cannot but confess that I have detected another. Browning
has, obviously, perceived that nothing but a larger Movement
on behalf of the Women will rescue our Norwood Duchesses
from their merciless ennui. *The Women's Movement*. Here
is our Gipsy—our Queen. Here is our Incantation : our
Charm : our Contagion.

And he has gone further ; and has noted the extraordinary
fact that to the outward eye—to the impatient scoffer, this
inspiring and inspired Movement takes the extraordinary
shape of a Passion for sharing in our *Examinations*.

---

[1] "My Friends and I," Julian Sturgis.

The Rescue, the Inspiration, the Magic—these present themselves before the Dukes and Duchesses of Putney in the disguise of a Competitive Examination. How beautiful is our Poet's treatment of this point ! He gives us the Gipsy witch. The shock at first sight. If a Competitive Examination could be conceived of as getting up and walking about our Earth, what other shape could it possibly assume ?

> " Under his nose (the Duke's)
>   The old witch peered up
> With her worn-out eyes (over reading),
>   Or rather eye-holes,
> Of no use now but to gather brine,
> And began a kind of level whine
>   (*Exactly ! the very picture of Viva-Voce*),
> Such as they used to sing to their viols
> When their ditties they go grinding
> Up and down with *nobody minding*."

So the Movement appears—in this uncanny disguise. And each Duke of Norwood looks at this

> " Sordid crone, bent well nigh double,"

and contrasts

> " The life of his lady, so flower-like and delicate,
> With the loathsome squalor of this old helicate."

Yes ! but within ! Within it is a different matter ! *Inside* the Lecture and the Schools, the Pass and the Plough. *Inside* lies the great secret of Escape—of Relief—of Liberty ! the Inspiration ! the Music that can prop up the stark letters of dry Learning. We think they have a strange fancy to grind for an *Examination*. But as we turn and look round sharply, we are surprised, as our friend in the poem was surprised :

> " The old witch has shot up a full head in stature,
> And the ignoble mien was wholly altered,
> And the face looked quite of another nature.
> And under her brow like a snail's horn newly
> Come out, as after the rain he paces,
> Two unmistakeable eye-points duly
> Live and aware looked out of their places."

And that is why our little ladies are found so strangely bewitched, sitting there between the knees of the Crone with faces upturned—

> " As if it were life their eyes were drinking
> From the crone's wide pair above, unwinking,
> Life's pure fire received without shrinking."

This is why at musty lectures their cheeks burn and their eyes glisten " As still they listen and they listen."

And yet—after all—it is only the *Exam.* Greats, or Mods or Smalls. We look, and—

> " Lo ! the crone is merely jabbering
> In the old style.
> Both her eyes have sunk
> Back to their pits."

This is obviously the plain and direct meaning of the Poet, and if any one presumes to doubt it, I would only plead that the Witch is much more like a Competitive Examination than she is like a Lover.

OXFORD, *Nov.,* 1886.

IV

MR. RUSKIN AND ROSE

"WHO that has ever seen him can forget John Ruskin ? How quaint the mingling of wistfulness in the countenance with the blue scarf and the frock coat, which made him look something between an old-fashioned nobleman of the 'Forties and an angel that had lost his way." [1]

The first person who ever kindled me on John Ruskin, that is to say on his personal history, was Lady Mount Temple. She was a " tutelary power in his life," his " Egeria," a kind of saint or goddess, illuminating and inspiring all that was best and greatest in him, very beautiful in every sense of the word, beautiful to look at, beautiful to know. Henry Cowper, her nephew, spoke of her to me as the most wonderful and beautiful personality he had ever met, the personification of Divine Love, more nearly an angel than a human being, yet most human in her relations with the sick and the suffering, the helpless and the sad. I remember the sense of being transported miles from this world's atmosphere when

[1] H. S. Holland.

with Lord and Lady Mount Temple in their house in London.

She was, by turns, his " Granny," because she took care of him and " aided him in his chief sorrow "; his " Isola Bella," " because she is so unapproachable, yet open on all sides to waifs of the waves and the world, claiming haven and rest in her sympathy." In the deep waters of perplexity and sadness that overwhelmed him, she was his confidante, his counsellor and his comfort.

It was Lady Mount Temple who first told me the story of Ruskin's marriage. He had nourished a deep attachment in boyhood to his cousin Adèle, and when she married, at the time when he was an Oxford undergraduate, he fell into a state of depression which affected him physically as well as mentally. Disease threatened his lungs ; mind and spirit were tinged with deepest melancholy.

His father and mother and his old nurse had taken up their residence at Oxford when the precious only son first became an undergraduate. They watched these symptoms with growing apprehension. They took him abroad and tried in every way to change the current of his thoughts. Their dearest wish, and that of their great friends, Mr. and Mrs. Gray, was to see the cherished son and the cherished daughter united in marriage, and both sets of parents facilitated and encouraged their companionship in every

way. The two became great friends, and, in course
of time, the father and mother suggested to their
son a closer union. The son had grown up with the
strongest sense of parental authority and of filial
obedience ; the fifth Commandment came, with him,
before all others in sacredness ; the relation of the
son with his father and mother was, from the be-
ginning, quite unique in its intimacy in spite of its
rigidity ; even at the age of forty he still wrote daily
to his parents. Serene and happy in the companionship of this most attractive young girl, he was quite
willing to accept the assurance of his father and
mother that it only needed the closer union for
affection to grow into love. In 1848 he married Effie
Gray, and their relations to each other continued to
be those of brother and sister. He was deeply
engrossed with every aspect of Nature and of Art,
such as found expression in his unique writings, and
the placid, even tenor of their outwardly joint lives
flowed calmly on. It was an unusual condition of
affairs, for his parents joined the newly married
couple before the honeymoon was over. Their son
was far more passionately wrapped up in his work
than in his wife, and at no time did their companionship quicken into any closer union. He sometimes
journeyed with his parents while she returned home
to Mr. and Mrs. Gray.

It was five years later (1853), when they both

took up their abode at Glenfinlas, in Scotland, that
matters approached a crisis. John Millais, the great
friend of Ruskin, and at that time in the meridian of
his glory as an artist, was living in their neighbour-
hood, and the intimate intercourse between the three
gradually changed their relations to one another. It
was not to be expected that the unnatural relations
subsisting between husband and wife could continue
indefinitely. That year Effie left her husband and
returned to her own home ; their marriage was
legally declared null and void, and just one year later
the wedding between Effie Gray and John Millais
took place.

As I listened to this story the words once spoken
to me by my own father came back to me : " Should
you ever hear any one blame Millais, or his wife, or
Mr. Ruskin, remember there was no fault ; there
was misfortune, even tragedy ; all three were
perfectly blameless."

There is no branch of the Catholic Church,
Anglican, Roman or Greek, that would acknowledge
a union such as the Ruskins' as a valid marriage. It
was perfectly natural that Effie and John Millais
should fall in love with one another, for there was
nothing but a purely nominal bar between them. It
seems well to make this absolutely clear, as, though
it is implied in the authorised " Life of Ruskin,"

there are many who think it was an ordinary case of
divorce. The great romance and tragedy of his life
was to come later.

It was towards the close of the year 1858 that Mr.
and Mrs. Latouche, then residing in London, wrote
to consult Mr. Ruskin about the education of their
children. They had been deeply impressed by his
books, and specially in drawing and painting were
they keen to give their little girls the most inspired
teaching they could find. Mr. Ruskin offered to
teach them drawing under his own direct super-
vision, and from this time, in London and in Ireland
—Harristown was their country home—he became
their master. The two sisters were aged thirteen and
nine when this strange fellowship began. Judging
from the first recorded letter from Rose [1], written
from abroad, at the age of nine, to her master six
months after he began to teach them, the awakening
and development of the child's mind must have been
quite phenomenal. He rejoiced in an extraordinary
number of nicknames, some most recondite in their
meaning, given him by the children—such as Archigosaurus and Kingfisher. But the ordinary name, St.
Crumpet, they bestowed upon him at the start. It
may have been suggested by the name they gave
their governess—the name of Bun—a nice, cosy,
friendly name, with which Crumpet made a charm-

[1] "Life of Ruskin," E. T. Cook.

ing pair. This grew into St. Crumpet or St. C.;
the latter is Lady Mount Temple's name for him, but
with her it signifies St. Chrysostom, the Golden-
mouthed.

NICE,[1]
Monday, March 18, 1859.

DEAREST ST. CRUMPET,—

I am so sorry—I *couldn't* write before, there wasn't
one bit of time—I am so sorry you were disappointed—I
only got yr letter yesterday (Sunday), and we only got to
Nice late on Saturday afternoon—So I have got up so early
this morning to try and get a clear hour before breakfast. . . .
So you thought of us, dear St. Crumpet, and we too
thought so much of you—Thank you very much for the
Diary letter ; it was so nice of you to write so long a one—I
have so much to tell you too Archigosaurus so I will begin
from Dover, and tell you what befel us up to Nice. . . .
Well we had a rough passage, but we sat on deck and didn't
mind—We thought and talked about you—Every great wave
that came we called a ninth wave and we thought how
pleasant it would be to sit in a storm and draw them, but
I think if you had wanted it done, I'd have tried to do it,
St. Crumpet—There was what do you think at the prow
of our steamer—yr brother Archigosaurus, an alligator, and
we said it was you—Well, so we got to Calais, breakfasted at
the Table d'Hôte there, and then began that weary railroad
journey from Calais to Paris—The scenery was just the same
all the way—I suppose you know it—Those long straight
rows of poplars cut even at the tops and flat uninteresting
country—I drew the poplars in perspective for you St.
Crumpet—We got to Paris on Friday evening and stayed

till Wednesday—No, I couldn't, I tell you, there wasn't one
bit of time, or do you think I would not have seized it
directly for I know yr thinking why didn't she write—
It's too long to say all we did and didn't do in Paris, so I'll
only tell you about the Louvre and Notre Dame. We went
to the Louvre. Oh St. Crumpet how we thought of you
there—How we looked and talked about the Titians you
told us to look at particularly the glass ball one and the
white Rabbit—Yes we did, all of us, think them so very
beautiful—I liked two portraits of Titian's of two dark
gentlemen with earnest eyes better than any, I think. We
thought his skins so very beautifully done and we looked
at the pinks at the corners of the eyes and thought of you
again St. Crumpet.

We liked the Veronese of the children playing with
the dog very much. I think one of them the most
prominent with dark eyes and not looking at the dog is
very beautiful. Why does Paul Veronese put his own family
in the pictures of sacred subjects I wonder ? I liked the
little puppy in the boy's arms trying to get away—The
statues in the Louvre I think most beautiful. Is it wrong
St. Crumpet, to like that noble Venus Victrix as well as
Titian ? If it is am I a hardened little tinner ? Oh but
they are so beautiful those statues there's one of a Venus
leaning against a tree with a Lacerta running up it—Notre
Dame they are spoiling as quick as they can by colouring
those grand old pillars with ugly daubs of green and yellow
etc. It is a bore saying all we thought of Paris, I must get
on to the mountains. . . . Don't be Kingfishery dear St.
Crumpet ; how good it was of you to give yr Turners that
you love so much to the Oxford Museum. From Paris we
started early on Wednesday morning and travelled all day

and all night in the train—Yes you would have said " Poor
Posie." I *was* bored. But we got over it very well—It was
so pleasant to be running after the sun (Don't be Kingfishery) and awaking at about 5 in the morning to see grey-
headed silvery olives and here and there pink perky peach
trees dancing among them—And there were groups of dark
cool cyprus trees pointing upwards, and hills and grey rocks
sloping to the sea. So we shook off our sleepiness . . . and
saw behind those peaks of craggy hills a pink smile coming
in the sky. So we watched and suddenly there rose (popped
wd be a better word for it really rose in one instant) such a
sun—" nor dim, nor red " (you know the verse). . . . It
was so beautiful—But I shocked Mama by saying " Jack
in the box " which woke Emily who declared of course
she had been wide awake and had seen it all. Why do people
always do that, St. Crumpet ? This was just before we
came to Marseilles. It had been snowing the day before
and it was nice to go to sleep and wake up in the summer. . . .
At Toulon it was like July—I don't like such heat. Trans-
plantation and scorching is too much for an Irish rose. . . .
The country was so beautiful some of it and towards
evening we saw snowy peaks, the mountains of Savoy. . . .
The next day we walked about two hours of the way over
the hills. You know what sort of a view there was at the top
and how one stands and stares and says nothing because
the words Grand—Glorious—Beautiful, etc., cannot in one
quarter express what one thinks. You the author of
M——P——s,[1] could describe it, Irish roses can't. But
I can tell you how my cousins the moorland roses nodded
at me as I passed and how they couldn't understand why
Irish hedge roses bloomed in July instead of March.

[1] " Modern Painters."

I can tell you how the fields were white with Narcissi, how the roads were edged with mauve-coloured anemones and how the scarlet anemones stood up in the meadows tantalising me in the carriage so much because I wanted to feel them. And there were myrtles (wild) growing close to the blue Mediterranean and Mama lay down on them by the seaside. . . . Well we got here (Nice) on Saturday evening and we climbed up an old Roman Amphitheatre and saw of all sunsets the most glorious. . . . Oh, St. Crumpet I think of you so much and of all your dearnesses to me :

I wish so very much that you were happy—God can make you so—We will try not to forget all you taught us. . . . I hope Mr. and Mrs. Ruskin are well now. Will you give them our love please and take for yourself as much as ever you please. It will be a great deal if you deign to take all we send you. I like Nice but I don't much like being transplanted except going home. I am ever your rose.

Postscript.

Yes, write packets—trunks, and we shall like them so much. Indeed I couldn't write before, I'll try to write again. You *must* see how we think and talk of you. rosie posie.

May not this letter stand as one of the most wonderful child's letters ever written—at nine years old. As Mr. Ruskin said of it afterwards, " There is not one sentence in which the child is thinking of herself." She guessed, she felt, she knew, just exactly what he was bearing, suffering, feeling. Her one and only thought was " Can I help him or give him any joy."

Here is another little letter written three years later, at the age of thirteen :—

I got your letter just as I was going out riding. So I could only give it one peep, and then tucked it into my riding-habit pocket and pinned it down, so that it could be talking to me while I was riding. I had to shut up my mouth so tight when I met Mama, for she would have taken it and read it if I'd told her, and it wouldn't have gone on riding with me. As it was, we ran rather a chance of me and pocket and letter and all being suddenly lodged in a stubble field, for Swallow (that's Emily's animal that I always ride now) was in such tremendous spirits about having your handwriting on his back that he took to kicking and jumping in such a way, till I felt like a Stormy Petrel riding a great wave, so you may imagine I could not spare a hand to unpin my dear pocket, and had to wait in patience, till Swallow had done " flying, flying South " and we were safe home again.

Rose was passionately religious and sometimes feared he wandered in what she called " By-path meadows." [1]

It is the day after Christmas Day and I have just got my Christmas letter ; and though I don't know your address, I have been wanting to write to you so much that I am answering it directly—and first St. C. you know you shouldn't write to me when you ought to be getting yourself warm ; couldn't you have thought of me just as well running up a hill and getting nice and warm, like a good St. Crumpet, than sitting cold writing ; for you know you needn't write to tell me you have not forgotten me, need you, St. C. ?

[1] " Pilgrim's Progress."

and yet I can't help saying I was looking for a letter, I wanted so much to know what you were doing and thinking this Christmas. . . . You know I only call " yowling " feeling like a dog with his nose up in the air outside a shut door, because some one has kicked, or perhaps because some one has not stroked you. Yowling is only for self ; I do not call it yowling to be sorry for those who are suffering . . . there is always something to be sorrowful about for other people—*sometimes* also a great deal to be yowlful about for self, and even in Christmas times. But I did not yowl about Harristown [1] . . . only just dreamt about home and our cats and the people, and that was somehow joined on to a dream about you. So our thoughts were crossing I suppose St. C., and I thought particularly the day before Xmas and Xmas day evening, is it not curious ? . . . I was sitting on my table opposite to the window, where I looked straight at the dark night, and one star Venus glowing in front. . . . I did not see Orion or any other star, only her. And then I was thinking of you ; it made me think of the guide of the wise men, His star in the East, only this shone in the West. She looked down so brightly over the gas lights as if it was intended we should see how much purer and brighter, though at such—such—a distance, is the Heavenly light if we would only look for it. . . . Yes, we have a strange Peace on earth, because earth or its inhabitants do not all of them like the Peace that our Prince can give, do not want it, do not believe in it. Some think that Pleasure is Peace and seek it for themselves ; some think that following Satan is Peace, and some think there is no Peace given on earth, that God gives work to do and strength to do it, sore with sorrow and with pain ; but peace is only in

[1] Her home in Ireland.

Heaven . . . but they are ready to give up their lives in His service, and live without joy, if it is His will. They are faithful noble souls, but though they could die for God, they are beaten back and tossed with the waves of temptation and sorrow ; they will not believe in the hope and joyful parts of Christianity and by rejecting God as the Comforter they reject all Peace. I believe we don't *believe* in that Peace rightly.

Alas, these letters, written before the full grace of maiden and womanhood had come to her, are all that remain of her correspondence with her loved master. After his death their love letters were reverently burned by Mr. Ruskin's executors, Mrs. Severn and Professor Norton. On a day in autumn they carried them to the garden, high above Brantwood, and gave them to the flames . . . Surely they ought rather to have buried them in a temporary grave, deep among the secrets of Mother Earth, for forty or fifty years !

Can we forgive it ? Can we bear to think of what the world has lost in the destruction of these love letters, possibly the most exquisite ever written in the English language ? In purity and passion they must have been unique. Can we pardon this burning, done in all love and reverence, yet possibly the most tragic incendiarism of our age ? From the fragments of her letters we have quoted, we can judge them to have been the sweetest ever penned, and we know from his unequalled writings what a height the letters must have reached under the influence of an overpowering passion.

It was when the charming child grew into her lovely girlhood that Mr. Ruskin gradually awoke to the knowledge that the enthusiastic devotion he felt for her could only signify one thing. No sooner had he discovered the real nature of his love, than he confessed it to Rose's parents. They had regarded him so much more in the light of their own friend that the idea came to them as a shock. Perfect freedom was all they asked for their child, and for this reason Mr. Ruskin left them for three years. Rose was to " come out " in the usual way, and was to be left unconscious of the passion she had aroused. The three years passed as three days in the life of the lover, so great was the love he bore her. At the end of that time her affections were still utterly free. Mr. Ruskin returned and revealed to Rose what was in his heart. In the same pure spirit of selflessness that breathes through her childish letters, in an impulse of overwhelming gratitude, she gave him her consent. Her first feeling was the great honour he had done her, her master and her guide, the inspiration of her youth—he who had awoken her from childhood's enchanted sleep and revealed to her the beauty and the wonder of the world. She found herself unable to resist the furnace of his love.

But it could not last. She loved him ; she revered

him—she was not in love with him. The conditions
of an engagement, so different to the restraint, the
delicacy, the reserve, of the relation between master
and pupil, jarred upon her sensitive nature, and the
engagement came to an end. The years that followed were years of poignant distress and difficulty
to both of them. In his absence, when the physical
nearness was removed, the spiritual attraction was
at its strongest. Remorse would seize her ; she was
maiming the life of one whom she admired and
revered above all other men, one to whom she owed
a debt that could never be repaid, even though she
were to give him her life. And again and again he
would return, ever feeling it an honour and a glory
to obey her slightest inclination, wish or whim.
And again the delicate spirit shrank. At length there
came a time when all her doubts and fears melted
away into " quietness and assurance for ever."
There then ensued a short period of ineffable happiness and calm. But illness seized her ; she suffered
acutely with brain fever, and the fragile, sensitive
life came to an end.

This deeply moving story was told me by Lady
Mount Temple, and I have tried to give it as it was
told to me.

The first of the letters we have quoted was kept
by Mr. Ruskin in his breast pocket between two

sheets of fine gold and carried with him wherever he went. The others he kept in a rosewood box.

Mr. Ruskin was never the same man again—her death was " the seal of a great fountain that can never ebb away." Henceforth it was ever his creed that grace and beauty and strength of character were gained by giving, more than by receiving love ; that a man who has not deeply loved can never attain the highest. To him all women were worshipful, no service was too hard, no love was too reverent. For him—

> Their feet had touched the meadows
> And left the daisies rosy.

By idealising them, by believing them to be queens in their gardens, he stimulated and inspired them to justify his faith in them.

There are but two children I can remember who can compare with this Irish Rose : Dr. Brown's " Pet Marjorie " and William Canton, author of that wonderful book, " The Invisible Playmate "—both imperishable memories—both recalling words used about another " half angel and half bird, the fluttering passion of the bird with the flashing purity of the angel."

V

TENNYSON AND LAURA TENNANT

September 8th to 21st, 1883

IN the autumn of 1883 we were suddenly invited
to a trial trip in the *Pembroke Castle*, a new
steamer of 4,000 tons. Within one week of Sir
Donald Currie's telegram, our party was actually
on board, my contribution being the Tennysons,
father and son, Arthur Lyttelton, and, at Herbert's
suggestion, Laura. Besides the Prime Minister and
the Poet Laureate, we had Constance Gladstone, Sir
Andrew Clark, Mr. Algernon West, Lord Dalhousie,
Sir Arthur Gordon,[1] and one or two friends invited
by our host.

The notes on this voyage Laura Tennant gave to
me will best give her own impressions. As to the
impressions of her made on our fellow-passengers,
there was variety, but unanimity on one point,
namely, that one and all underwent a change in their
opinion concerning her. Perhaps this will best be
realised by a quotation from one of their letters

[1] Afterwards Lord Stanmore.

written to me some time afterwards. I will only
say the writer was not a woman.

" I saw Miss Tennant for the first time when she
came on board at Barrow. The circumstances in
which she did so were such as to bring into the
greatest prominence all that was least attractive in
her outward characteristics. She had accidentally
been left behind, and she came on board excited by
her adventure. She talked more, faster, and in a
higher key than at any subsequent time ; she laughed
much and unmusically. I must frankly confess that
what I then saw and heard prejudiced me strongly
against her. That repose was an essential indication
of good breeding and its absence a fault for which
nothing could atone, were instincts deeply ingrained
in me, and it must be admitted that there was much
about Miss Tennant likely to prove startling to any
one entertaining such views. My thoughts that first
evening of our voyage were somewhat to this effect :
' Good heavens ! that young woman will spoil the
cruise. I shall make some excuse and leave them
at Oban.' But the very next day I had some talk
with her, accidentally, on deck. She was no longer
noisy ; her conversation was *très spirituelle*, and,
though repose might be absent, she was decidedly
uncommon. As day by day passed I discovered more
and more that was attractive, and as she displayed
more freely the earnestness and goodness of a very

transparent character, I found distaste rapidly giving way to real liking and esteem.

" Great unselfishness, an extremely original and independent cast of thought, and an earnest longing to benefit others (a different thing from unselfishness), were, I think, the positive qualities which most struck me ; and, in addition, there was a nameless charm and winningness which fully justified Lord Tennyson's calling her, as he habitually did, ' The Little Witch.' The time we passed together was short, but I look on the intercourse as a thing not to be forgotten, and on the acquaintance I made with her as a piece of rare good fortune. The only letter I ever received from her has been treasured up among those which I shall never destroy. . . .

" I have just read over, with infinite disgust, what I have written about Miss Tennant. It does not convey in the least what I wish it to convey, for it gives no idea of her peculiar and indefinable charm."

This will show that there was a good deal in her looks and ways which did not at first seem to fit on to what one discovered later ; in fact, there was something which, at first sight, appeared to belong to a different stamp of character, and, knowing little of her antecedents, it was difficult to make enough allowance. Sailors and all, while greatly attracted and amused by her liveliness, at first thought and spoke lightly of her. There were even some on board so matter-of-fact, so unimaginative, as seriously to misjudge her ; they failed to see that the freedom with which she approached both men and women alike in reality came from unconsciousness of the difference between them.

She had the grace and quickness and mischievousness of a kitten. Her sense of fun, of antithesis, sometimes led her into daring expressions, dangerously near forbidden ground. A madcap, a dare-devil, she was literally brimming with *joie de vivre ;* nothing was safe in heaven or earth, or under the earth, from the sallies of her wit. One trembles to think what would have happened had it not been for the restraining influence of her spiritual side. She never seemed capable of being bored, distributed herself pretty equally all round, and talked to bores (we were not without them) with the same eagerness and animation as to poets and premiers ; could strike sparks out of the deadest wood, and make the heaviest natures shine ; she had any number of *tête-a-têtes,* but at meals kept the whole party alive ; never poached on other people's preserves or spoiled anybody else's game. I never knew anybody with such unique powers of super-attraction so shine in this way. It was generosity carried to a pitch I have never seen before. She was ready and willing to sacrifice her-self for anybody. She would give away the most precious things she possessed if she once thought they would give pleasure to others. I remember I never even discovered how well she played, she so entirely, during that fortnight, appropriated the pianoforte to me.

Anything like rebuke she accepted with utter humbleness and remorse. Her penitence was so disarming that very quickly the tables were turned and one was learning from her. " I lie awake and think of it all, and how wrong I have been and how wretched I am, and then the next day I go and do something just as bad, and *I might as well have slept*." She was

> Active, stirring, all on fire,
> Could not rest, could not tire.

Extraordinarily brilliant in conversation, though apt to be run away with, the life and soul of the company one minute, and then the next she would be an altered being, with that curious, indescribably weird, far-off look in her eyes, so sad, so wistful, her face small and pale and pitiful as a suffering child's, you could cry simply by looking at her. And at those times I used to feel she did not belong to us : the little body was here, frail and white, but the soul, it seemed to escape. Her eyes were wonderful when she looked like that and quite unearthly. We felt their mystic power. I remember this look on her face while listening to the speech at Kirkwall. The freedom

of the city was conferred on both " Grand Old Men."
Tennyson growled ferociously, and said nothing
should induce him to make a speech. Mr. Gladstone promised to include his thanks, which he did
in a beautiful allusion to the eternity of the poet's
power and influence as compared with the politi-
cian's. After which it turned out that Tennyson,
like a spoilt child, was annoyed at being taken at
his word and was ready to speak for himself ! He
seemed, in talking to Laura, greatly surprised and
perplexed at not receiving everywhere we landed a
quite equal degree of enthusiastic homage as the
Prime Minister.

Our cruise lasted altogether just a fortnight,
leaving Barrow September 8th, dawdling up the
west coast of Scotland, crossing from Kirkwall to
Christiansund, a wonderful moonlight night. I
remember a gleaming path of silver across the
water. " Like a great river rushing to the City
of God," said Tennyson, as he watched spellbound.
Pacing up and down the deck he and Laura were
discussing the poet's various methods of greeting.
He appeared to think kisses always acceptable.
" You will not dare kiss M——'s hair next time
we pass her ? " said Laura. " Shouldn't I ? You
will see." They passed, and Laura triumphed.
" I could not," he said, " the sun was kissing
her."

It was all rather like a play, the couples that paced up and down the deck, or sat in snug nooks protected by boats, the moonlight making it very romantic. Tennyson used to read to us in the smoking-room. One day, as he reached the last words of " The Promise of May "—" And the papers called that a failure ; why, it's a perfect gem." This he said in the most naïve way, and took our silence for consent.

After Norway we went to Copenhagen, dined at Fredensborg, and received a royal party of fifty next day at luncheon on board, starting for England as soon as the last royal barge had left us and landing at Gravesend, Saturday, September 22nd.

Here follow extracts from the notes Laura wrote at the time, and which she gave to me :—

On board the " Pembroke Castle," off Jura and Isla, 9th September, 10.30 p.m.

Sailed from Barrow yesterday about 4 p.m. . . . Mr. Gladstone and Tennyson and other lesser human beings, I being the less-est. My first introduction to Tennyson was this :—standing looking at Scawfell, I said to Herbert " Isn't it lovely ? " Tennyson walked up. " Yes, and cold too, like some women I know." And then silently walked on in a hat ! ! and a cloak ! ! ! I note the ideal Poet's garments. Later on he and I sat on the bridge and talked of mesmerism —Blake—Mrs. Kingsford—Buddhism, etc. He told me this story. In Scotland he was once sent for by a doctor, to come and mesmerize a lady in great pain, a mutual friend. Tennyson had never mesmerized before, but he succeeded and put her into a long painless sleep. Later on the same lady suffered acute pain in one of her eyes, and the doctor asked Tennyson to breathe on her. With one breath he again put her into a state of unconsciousness ; yet this marvellous power had never been previously exercised. I sat next to Hallam, his son, at dinner last night and got on well. I think him unattractive, and yet I like him and feel there is a beyond in him which is a great comfort. Then Arthur Lyttelton, a Parson, is here, beautiful, I think, inside and out. A fine head and so unself-conscious. . . . Mrs. Gladstone is a darling—the Premier, of course, is the Holiest of Holies. I have heard him quote English, French, Italian and Greek. He and I walked a little last night and he talked about Scott. He thinks historical novels are worth any amount of social novels. . . .

Sept. 10th.   Off Oban.

Glorious day—never saw anything so beautiful . . . I am immensely happy and having the greatest fun in the world. Tennyson and I get on like a Palace on Fire and he calls me the " Little Witch." He is kind and gruff and big . . . most people quail before him. The G.O.M. I look upon as too sacred to talk to. . . . Oh ! Tennyson was so funny to-day— he asked me to kiss him ! which I promptly did and would any day ! I love him. We talked of Swinburne and Rossetti—of fame—and cabbages and kings. He said to me this morning—" I find it much harder to realise matter than spirit " . . . I understand so well what he means, and would much sooner doubt my body than my soul. . . . It is so wonderful living with two Kings on board—Bless them !

Wednesday, Sept. 11th. Tobermory.

This has been the most lovely day of my life, the bluest, sweetest day, with an opal sea and baby islands, and ruby heather and golden ferns, and seals and porpoises, and sails of Indian red, and the sun kissing the world, and the waves clasping one another and the sea gulls spreading their white wings westward, startled from their rocky home by the coming of our enchanted boat. We sailed past Eigg, Muck, Rum, Skye, this morning, and up Loch Hourn and now are anchored here for the night. Tennyson has been at his best. He read to us " The Two Voices " and to-night half " The Promise of May." He reads beautifully, like a Cathedral Bell. I mended a great hole in his coat this afternoon. He had put his pipe in his pocket lighted, so burnt a big hole over his heart. He said I had looked at it ! Sir William Harcourt and Loulou dined with us. Sir Donald brought me a pansy from Tennyson, with his thanks that I had not left him wholly (I was not at his table). . . . Mr. West's eyes grow bluer every day . . . Hallam grows too . . . not blue, but nice.

Saturday, Sept. 15th. Between Christiansund and Copenhagen.

It was settled the day before yesterday that we were to go to Norway and from thence to Denmark. . . . I told Tennyson I must leave them. " Nonsense, little witch, you must not go, you are the Life of the Party—Gladstone and I will sign a Round Robin to prevent you going." . . . It is the first time, and will probably be the last, I shall be asked to do something to please a Poet Laureate. . . . I am so happy, tho' I had a fit of the blue devils yesterday. . . . I have never had such a week since St. Moritz, August,

1880. . . . Tennyson told me I was a mixture of woman and child, which is the nicest, rarest thing in the world. We talk of every sort of thing—of Poets (Pope, by the way, he calls a distinct Poet, Wordsworth he puts very high— some things quite perfect, Keats he puts before Shelley, Rossetti before Swinburne), of Life and Fame, and Death and Power and the Future. He read the " Northern Cobbler," " The Grandmother," " Rizpah," " The Children's Hospital," " Ask me no more," and " The Echo dying, dying, dying." His voice is beautiful, sonorous and pathetic, he broke down reading " The Grandmother." . . .

Sunday, Sept. 16th. Copenhagen.

We arrived here about 5.30 p.m. Here we lie anchored, surrounded by Danish, Russian and English ships of all sorts. We passed the Imperial Yacht, Russian, all white and gold, and were told the Czar was in the little steamer we passed as we came into dock. I believe there are eight crowned heads here. Some of the men landed—Mary and I didn't because of Evening Service. It was a glorious night, a moon clear and full, gazing at her own pale face in the waters beneath, and wreathed in a tawny garland of cloud. . . . Gladdy and Auntie Pussy (Mrs. Gladdy) have to dine at the Palace to-morrow, and Tennyson too—I believe the poor old man dreads it. Yesterday, driving into the country from Christiansund, we had Arthur Lyttelton in our carriage, whom I like immensely ; and Herbert, whom I have always thought a really fine good character, and of whom I think better every day ; and Algy West—he has a soul " all to himself," as the children say. The scenery, I should say, very typical Norway, green slopes and firs and pines and rocks and grass, and a broad black river, and little

red-roofed houses painted white or yellow, and flowers and
Virginia Creepers, and yellow-haired children and fainter
haired women, and creamy ponies with classic manes like
the Elgin Marbles.

Copenhagen. Tuesday, Sept. 18th, 4 p.m.

Two hours ago I was in a crowd of human beings, or is
it too familiar to speak of Kings and Queens and Counsellors
and a sprinkling of Imperial Majesties as human beings?
It was a curious experience—I sitting by the King of Denmark's brother, one door off the Queen of Greece. At my
back sat the Emperor of all the Russias, next Mrs. Gladdy,
the Queen of Denmark, the King and his two daughters,
the Empress of Russia and the Princess of Wales. Prince
Eddy and the three Princesses, his sisters, and a dozen
children besides, altogether forty to fifty Royalties. Interesting to see the Czar and Czarina and wondering how long
they will sit on their thrones, and which will be blown up
first—a ghastly thought and a ghastly state of things. The
Czar said he would rather be King of Denmark than Emperor
of Russia. Our Princess looked lovely as ever. Tennyson
read to them in the tiny smoking-room, between the Empress
and the Princess of Wales and patted them just as he does
us. I wonder he did not embrace them. Among all the
crowned heads, Gladstone is King of Kings. . . . We saw
the Thorwaldsen Museum and the Apostles and the Lord
Christ, and the Northern Antiquities, all shown by Professor
Herbst himself. To-day I have seen the corpse of a young
man of twenty, three thousand years old, lying there in his
open coffin grim and black . . . a fine well-developed
forehead, comparing well with the brows of to-day.

Last night six of the party dined at Fredensborg, three

hours distant from Copenhagen by train. They dined at
6 p.m. a hundred and twenty, all the Royal children there.
M. clad in black velvet and my jewels and fanning herself
with my fan. . . . She and I talked last night in my cabin
until two. . . . Every night I vow I will wake up different
and every morning I wake up the same. . . . Am I a
malicious witch, as Tennyson asked me, or am I a good
witch ? Anyhow M. is a far more " collected " spirit and
a better balanced mind. I wish I had half her qualities,
which are rare ones, I think, bless her.

Laura went off to Scotland and sent to each of her
fellow-travellers a small white " Hamlet "—" in
memory of Elsinore."

I have thought a great deal about it all [she wrote], and
it looks quite lovely. I have been reading about Fredensborg.
Did you see Caroline Matilda's prayer (sister of George *III*.
and wife of Christian *III*.), written with a diamond upon a
window : " O ! keep me innocent, make others great."

VI

"HERE'S ME"

" Two men looked out through prison bars—the one saw mud, the other stars."

AND so it will always be ; some quality within determines what the vision will be. But to those who see stars will be given the most joy in life, and it is they, moreover, who will give to others the most stimulus as well as the most fun. Those, on the other hand, who see, or think they see, mud in the " Autobiography of Margot Asquith," and who, after only reading or hearing the least discreet extracts from her book, resolve not to soil their eyes by reading it, will miss something of an invigorating wind blowing through the dusty corners of their souls. It has been often said that Mrs. Asquith has given a false and even disgraceful picture of modern society, or, rather, of what are called the upper classes. But where does the public really go for information, how do people form their opinions of society, what are the sources from which they gather knowledge ? Do not its thousands, possibly its millions, gather their information chiefly from the Press ? From the shilling shockers, the vicious novels, from the stage, the paragraphs in the Court Circular, from the *causes célèbres* that, in these days, occupy far more space than the things that make history ? Glance casually one day at your morning paper, and your eye may light on a column headed " Fashions in Paris." The impression you gather from it will be that the " smart set " are governed by two passions only : one, to wear the minimum, and two, to spend the maximum, on their own persons. In a neighbouring column, in large print, you may read : " The Earl of ——, who was divorced last year, was yesterday married at a registry office to Lady ——, who was divorced last week." Only the other day, ten or twelve portraits of ladies and gentlemen (so called) occupied the first page of a daily illustrated paper. Were they noted for some deed of valour, for some conspicuous gift of intellect or character, for any distinction of merit, beauty of form, of countenance, or of conduct ? No—the reason of their being exhibited to the public was because of their approaching presence in the Divorce Court. And from the circulating library you proceed to read the highly-spiced Diaries of Wilfrid Blunt and of Colonel à Court Repington. Besides all this, there is the idle gossip, the hinted scandal, that filters through a score of mouths, gradually swelling in volume in proportion as it loses in accuracy. For th is class—and who shall say how large a proportion of the community it represents ?—the book will come as something of the nature of a tonic, of a health-giving breeze.

It is said that " The Autobiography of Margot Asquith " came to pass in this wise.

" Can you give me a thousand pounds ? " said Mrs. Asquith one day to her husband.

" No—not even a thousand pence."

" Then may I write a book ? " she said.

" Yes ; on condition you do not ask me to read it."

A year later, on the day the book appeared, Mr. Asquith read it in one flash.

He quickly ran upstairs. " Margot," he said, " it is a masterpiece ; the little mistakes do not matter "—and the eyes of both were full of tears.

In these pages will be found no scandals, no hints or innuendoes, no shadowy lights or whispered flirtations. The atmosphere is nowhere unhealthy—all is exhilarating, open, alive, alert ; early rising, athletic sports or games, *joie de vivre*, pranks and fun, escapades innumerable, perilous to life and limb. The autobiographer is no respecter of persons ; to her a prince and a pauper, a Prime Minister or a ploughboy, will be of equal value so long as the character or personality impresses or attracts her.

The chief business of the autobiographer is to reveal herself, and probably this has never yet been accomplished with so complete an unself-consciousness and *naïveté*.

" I think it must be unusual," writes one who is not acquainted with the author but through her book, " for any one so egotistical, to be so penetrating and so ingenuous."

Instead of being prim and narrow-minded, may we not give play to our natural instincts and let ourselves be glad of so honest a self-revelation ? We see her in her strength and in her weakness, in her loves and in her hates, in her joys and in her sorrows, in the endearing and enduring qualities of her character. We have, too, her faults and her foibles, her restlessness, her lack of proportion, her rash judgments, her charming inaccuracies, relentlessly and with perfect frankness detailed before us.   The title of the book might well have been " Here's me "—the words that sprang from her lips when, as a vivacious infant, she danced into the crowded drawing-room. It is a real " human document "—literally human nature poured out upon the pages. She has not changed, though, as is obvious, the richness and variety of her life's experiences have added vastly to the interest of her personality—egotistic, yes, but not self-conscious. Not " What do they think of me ? " which would signify self-consciousness, but " What do I think of them ? " which is egotism. She is the same now as she was then—a madcap, a dare-devil, impetuous, impatient, fearless, generous, with much wit and little wisdom, quick in insight, rapid in repartee.

It may be interesting to quote a letter written to me nearly forty years ago by the High Priest of the group of friends she describes as " the Souls." The letter might have been written to-day :—

Perhaps you hardly make sufficient allowance for a nature whose faults and whose merits alike arise from an absolute and really " phenomenal " naturalness, a naturalness which knows no rules and recognises no conventions, which therefore sometimes induces her to violate the canons of perfect taste, and do and say things which had infinitely better be left unsaid and undone, but which nevertheless has in it the merit of sincerity and veracity, and is, I think, quite unalloyed with any kind of meanness.

This letter was written in 1886, at the time when, as Margot Tennant, she joined what had been an intimate and exclusive little group of friends, originally formed about fifteen years earlier, at Hawarden, in 1870.

As I have written elsewhere, when Laura Tennant appeared upon the scene, shortly after she went with Mr. and Mrs. Gladstone on their famous trip to Denmark in 1883, she simply romped in carrying everything and everybody before her, and drawing after her half the stars of the firmament. The atmosphere became, later on, one of rampant impulsiveness, bordering on recklessness, or, more accurately, headlongness. Constant introspection, constant criticism and competition, constant advertisement of its results, a passion for repartee, for scoring, for being a success, together with brilliant mental gifts, a magic power of insight, genuine intellectual hunger, no serious ill-nature, and, generally speaking, real warmth and generosity of heart.

And what a spoiling life it was ! How few of us could have stood it sanely. Nearly all the gifts, nearly all the graces, all the luck, looks, love, charm, talent, money, sense and sensibility, breadth of outlook and sunshine of heart—all this was showered wholesale upon this fortunate family. From over the Border they raided England, capturing all they encountered ; they came, they saw, they conquered, reigning over kings and queens, poets and statesmen, doctors and divines, young men and maidens, old men and children—all were at their feet. And with the intoxication of this *succès fou*, in spite of rashness bordering on recklessness, daring situations and adventures, they had the power of keeping the bounds that really matter. A gallant gentleman can snatch up the dripping girl, dripping from a tumble into the river, fly up the stairs, and, depositing his fairy burden upon her couch, is happy to leave her with a deferential kiss upon the hand. Here is the real secret of their success : they knew where and when to stop—thus far and no further. Let us all read, but let us not all copy, and more especially those weaker vessels who have not the faculty, and maybe not the wish, to use the curb.

The book has been furiously assailed with almost savage spite, sometimes from jealousy or political prejudice, sometimes from wounded susceptibilities. But her very enemies have been hoist with their own petard ; they have given her a niche in the Temple of Fame, they have endowed the book with a gift it perhaps does not quite deserve—the gift of immortality. The historic mind is possibly inclined to exaggerate the importance of its inaccuracies ; but how often it happens that a more vivid impression of the truth is given by a rapid flash of description than by the most exact and laborious accuracy of detail. It has been well said that she has a power of sudden vividness that is like the switching on of electric light.

" All good men," wrote Mr. Edmund Gosse, " and most women, if they have the power to admire, will unite in praise."

And another distinguished man of letters,[1] commenting on the fact that she had known most of the interesting minds in the most interesting time of our

---

[1] John Masefield.

history, continues—she has " all this equipment of language, analysis, variety of interest, gaiety, surety of mind, mental memory, and, the much rarer thing, memory of emotion, as well as the colour of having been a participant, and the zest of being a partisan, to a degree rare in writers, very rare in historians, and not known hitherto in English memoir writers."

And as to the accusation of vanity, of conceit, after all, which is the most egotistical—to paint your own portrait or to commission some one else to paint it ? To describe yourself with the utmost honesty, or to conceal yourself behind the praise and approbation, or even flattery, of your correspondents ? The latter is infinitely more subtle, and is more attractive, because of its apparent reticence and modesty ; it will very likely produce a more winning picture. In neither case would the author set out to praise herself—in both cases self-esteem is accidental. As an illustration may I give the following personal experience ?

The writer of this review was one day in the bookshop belonging to the Oxford University Press in Paternoster Row. She overheard an American lady with a strong nasal twang ask for " Little Helen's Burden." Seeing the attendant was evidently puzzled, I suggested "Little Henry and his Bearer " (Mrs. Sherwood), and then, pointing to a gentleman examining books under the guidance of

Mr. Frowde, very nearly added, "That is Lord Rosebery, and I am Mr. Gladstone's daughter," but from pure self-consciousness, of course, kept silence. If it had been Mrs. Asquith, the one and only impulse that would have moved her would have been the delight that could be so easily given to the American lady.

How often it is a misplaced consciousness of self, not modesty or humility, that militates against being purely natural. What masterpieces, what priceless treasures we should have lost in the past, if their authors had refrained from writing them through self-consciousness—the Confessions of St. Augustine, the classic description by De Quincey of his little sister's death. Has any stepmother ever written, at any period, with more tenderness and unselfish appreciation of her stepchildren and their mother than Mrs. Asquith? And as to those indefinable qualities, dignity, reticence, taste, what two people will ever agree in saying precisely what they mean, or in establishing a standard by which they can be interpreted? There is no doubt there are lapses, though there might be some difference of opinion with regard to them. But there can be no question as to the book being one of the most brilliant of our own day, and especially in studies of character. Mrs. Asquith has extraordinary *insight*, but she is perhaps without the more subtle gift of

intuition. There is a striking passage in a letter of
Lord Acton's, which we will quote here to show
what Mrs. Asquith is not. Lord Acton describes
George Eliot's marvellous faculty of understanding
all varieties of human nature, " reading the diverse
hearts of men, of creeping into their skin, of watching
the world through their eyes," and, once possessed
of this equipment, " recovering her own independence, and exposing scientifically and indifferently
the soul of "—and here follows a list of the per-
sonalities of those George Eliot has thus presented
in her writings.

Mrs. Asquith sees not with the eyes of others, but
with her own eyes. Her own personality is too strong
to allow her to creep into the skin of others, to feel
with their hearts, to think with their minds. And
this she honestly confesses when she speaks of her
inability to know what will hurt or wound, whether
her friends or her enemies. She can put herself into
them, but, though inside them, she remains herself ;
she cannot identify herself with their personality.
Great and conspicuous as are her intelligences, she
is, so to say, without that sixth sense. As well may
a blind man be blamed for falling over the furniture
as condemn her for being unable to see with the eyes
of others. No doubt it produces a certain lopsided-
ness in her character. Who shall say ? But this can
be no excuse for the cruel misunderstanding that has

prevailed. I have heard on the best authority that
more than one man lying in the valley of the shadow
of death has written to her, after reading her book,
to express his deep contrition for having so seriously
misjudged her, and to confess that his disapproval
has turned into admiration.

Let us take her largely, generously, and, above all
things, let us cultivate our own sense of proportion,
of values ; in short, of humour. Possibly we may
not be aware of any one belonging to us who would
have written this book. But the real question is
" Could they ' " not " Would they ? " Why not
start by asking ourselves the question—" How have
we used our own opportunities, our own gifts and
graces ? How far have we made the best use of
them ? Could we have had the wit to write this
book ? "

Two gracious extracts from letters written to her
in her maiden days by George, Lord Pembroke, and
Benjamin, Dr. Jowett, may close this review, as a
proof of how deeply her friendship was valued by
the best of men, even while they include some words
of warning :—

" Keep the outer borders of your heart free from garish
flowers and wild useless weeds, so that when your Fairy
Godmother turns the Prince's footsteps your way, he may
not, distrusting your nature and only half guessing at the
treasure within, tear himself reluctantly away and pass

sadly on without perhaps your ever knowing how near he had been."

The second, especially, we may all read and take to heart :—

" Child, why don't you make a better use of your noble gifts ? . . .   The higher we rise, the more self-discipline, self-control and economy is required of us.   It is a hard thing to be in the world but not of it, to get rid, not of wit and good humour, but of frivolity and excitement, to live selfless according to the Will of God.   And yet you do not do anything wrong—only what other people do, but with more success.   And you are very faithful to your friends. . . . And so, God bless you ! "

INDEX

INDEX

WAGGETT, Father Philip, S.S.J.E., on Dr. Holland, 92–5

Wales, Princess of, 129

Warre, Dr., 82

Webster, 28, 29

Wellesley, 28

West, Sir Algernon, 119, 127–8

Westcott, Bishop, 53, 58, 64

Westminster Abbey, 27, 30, 84

Westminster, Duke of, at St. Deiniol's, 48

White Cross League, The, 71

Windham, 28

Wood, Hon. F. (afterwards Meynell), 62